Dear Older Me
A Memoir *of Sorts*

Dr. Constance Santego

Maximillian Enterprises
Kelowna, BC

Dear Older Me: A Memoir of Sorts

Copyright © 2025 by Constance Santego.

Copy Editor & Interior Design: Constance Santego
Book Layout: ©2017 BookDesignTemplates.com

Ordering Information:
Quantity sales. Special discounts are available on quantity purchases by corporations, associations, and others. Contact the "Special Sales Department" at the address below for details.

Trade Paperback ISBN: 978-1-990062-73-5
eBook ISBN 978-1-990062-74-2
Created and published In Canada. Printed and bound in the United States of America

First Edition
Published by Maximillian Enterprises
Kelowna, BC
Canada
www.constancesantego.ca

ALSO BY DR. CONSTANCE SANTEGO

NOVELS

Illegitimate Grace

Okanagan Trilogy:

Beneath the Vineyards
Under the Okanagan Sun
Guardian of the Lake

The Nine Spiritual Gifts Series:
Journey of a Soul – (Vol 1 Michael)
Language of a Soul – (Vol 2 Gabriel)
Prophecy of a Soul – (Vol 3 Bath Kol)
Healing of a Soul – (Vol 4 Raphael)
Miracles of a Soul – (Vol 5 Hamied)
Knowledge of a Soul – (Vol 6 Raziel)
Wisdom of a Soul – (Vol 7 Uriel)
Faith of a Soul – (Vol 8 Pistis Sophia)

NONFICTION
The Intuitive Life, The Gift Of Prophecy, Third Edition
Fairy Tales, Dreams And Reality… Where Are You On Your Path? Second Edition
Your Persona… The Mask You Wear
Archangel Michael's Soul Retrieval Guide
Tesla And The Future Of Energy Medicine
Beyond Tesla: *Advancing The Science Of Energy Healing*
Tesla's Code: *Mastering Energy, Frequency, And Creative Power*
Beyond The Mind: *Harnessing The Power Of Astral Projection For Creative Awakening*
Bend, Don't Break: *Finding Your Way Back To Abundance*
Ring Therapy: *A Guide To Healing And Balance*
Ring Therapy Pocket Guide
Floraopathy™: *The Art And Science Of Vibrational Healing With Essential Oils*
Dear Older Me: *A Memoir… Of Sorts*
It's Just Like Poker: *A Spiritual Guide To Playing The Cards Life Deals You*
Signs And Meanings: *What The Feet Reveal About Health, Stress, And The Body's Story*
Auricions: *Unlocking Subconscious Healing Through Quantum Medicine*
More Than Bloodlines: *A Companion Book To Auricions*

REIKI WISDOM, SERIES:

Angelic Lifestyle, a Vibrant Lifestyle
Angelic Lifestyle 42-Day Energy Cleanse
Reiki and the Power of The Joint Points: *Unlocking Energy Pathways for Healing* (Vol I)
Reiki and Karmic Healing: *Releasing Patterns From Past Lives* (Vol II)
Reiki and the Five Elements (Vol III)
Secrets of a Healer, Magic Of Reiki
The Reiki Master's Manual

SECRETS OF A HEALER, SERIES:
Magic Of Aromatherapy (Vol I)
Magic Of Reflexology (Vol II)
Magic Of The Gifts (Vol III)
Magic Of Muscle Testing (Vol IV)
Magic Of Iridology (Vol V)
Magic Of Massage (Vol VI)
Magic Of Hypnotherapy (Vol VII)
Magic Of Reiki (Vol VIII)
Magic Of Advanced Aromatherapy (Vol IX)
Magic Of Esthetics (Vol X)
The Reiki Master's Manual (Vol XI)

ADULT COLORING JOURNALS

SERIES-ZEN COLORING:
Quantum Energy and Mindful Living Journal (Vol 1)
Reiki Energy Journal (Vol 2)
Nine Spiritual Gifts Journal (Vol 3)
I Forgive Journal (Vol 4)

FOR CHILDREN
I am Big Tonight. I Don't Need the Light

COOKBOOK
My Favorite Recipes, with a Hint of Giggle

BUISNESS
Scaling Beyond 6 Figures: *Strategies For Health & Wellness Professionals*
How To Use ChatGPT For Authors: From Idea To Published Book

Dedication

For the one inside me
who never stopped believing—
even when the world stopped listening.

For every child who was told to be quiet,
to behave, to grow up too soon…

And for every adult still learning
how to come home to themselves.

This is for you.
This is for *us*.

"Shift Happens... Create Magic!"
—Dr. Constance Santego

Preface

For the One Who Still Wonders If It's Too Late to Begin Again

This isn't the book I set out to write.
It began as a whisper—something soft, something unfinished—
until I realized it was *me* calling from within my own past. Not
for answers, but for reconnection.

I didn't know at the time that this would become my memoir.
Not in the traditional sense, but in a way that feels more honest
to who I am:
A collection of letters, memories, and truths from my younger
self to the woman I've become—and to the ones still searching.

Each page is a reflection of moments I lived through:
some tender, some turbulent, all transformative.
And in writing them, I began to see the magic I had buried…
the innocence I thought I'd lost…
the truth I had silenced to survive.

I wrote this for myself—
but I'm sharing it for you.

Because maybe you've forgotten parts of yourself too.
Maybe you've learned to be responsible, capable, polished, and
quiet—
but you ache for the wild, curious, knowing version of you that
came before.

These letters are my offering.
They are not written to give advice, but to open a doorway.
To help you remember. To stir something real.
To let you know you're not alone.

You may cry.
You may laugh.
You may see parts of your own story in mine.

If this book awakens something buried,
triggers old pain, or inspires a quiet "me too,"
then it's doing what it came here to do.

Because the past doesn't disappear.
It waits—
not to haunt us,
but to hand us the pieces we once dropped.

This is me picking them up.
This is me remembering.
This is *Dear Older Me*.

Welcome.

"We do not outgrow our childhood.
We carry it quietly—waiting for us
to remember
who we were before the world told
us who to be."

Dear Older Me

A Memoir...*of Sorts*

Remember Who We Were

Dear Reader, What Is a Memoir—And Why This One?

A memoir isn't just a collection of memories.
It's not a diary.
It's not a timeline of events, neatly recorded and bound.

A memoir is a *bridge*.
Between the person I was
and the person I've become.
Between my lived moments
and your quiet reflections.

It's a story shaped by emotion,
guided by truth,
and offered in the hopes that something within it
resonates with *you.*

People write memoirs to make sense of the life they've lived—
to look back and find meaning in the mess,
light in the shadows,
and courage in the decisions that shaped them.

We write them to say:
*This is where I've been. Maybe it helps you understand where
you are.*

What makes this memoir different?

I didn't write this because I've figured it all out.
I wrote it because I'm still learning.
Still healing.
Still becoming.

It's not just one story—it's many.
Snapshots of love and loss.
Choices I questioned.
Dreams I chased.
Moments that cracked me open
and made me more *me*.

I've been a mother, a wife, a healer, an entrepreneur, a dreamer.
But more than anything—I've been *human*.

And if you're reading this, maybe you've felt some of these
things too.
Maybe your story doesn't look exactly like mine,
but the emotions echo:
longing, hope, confusion, clarity, rising again.

This memoir isn't just about my past.
It's about what's still possible.
For me.
For you.

Thank you for walking this journey with me.
May it inspire you to honor your own.

With all my heart,
Constance Amoraa Santego

Dear Reader,

AS I have said, this isn't just a memoir.

It's an invitation—into my story, yes—but more than that, into *yours.*

As you turn these pages, you may feel echoes of your own past rising to the surface. A memory you tucked away. A feeling you once dismissed. A truth you forgot you knew.

Let them come.

Some of what you read might stir something tender.
It may feel raw, or too close for comfort.
But that's not a flaw—it's the medicine.
Because healing doesn't always arrive as soft light. Sometimes, it comes in recognition.

You may find yourself saying:
"I thought I was the only one who felt that way."
Or "I didn't realize how much I needed to hear this."
Or simply… "Me too."

This book was written to remind you of the voice you may have forgotten—
not the loud one shaped by expectation, but the quiet one beneath.
The curious one.
The courageous one.
The one that still believes in joy, in magic, in second chances.

You don't need to have lived the same life to feel what's here.
These letters were written from one soul to another.
Not to fix you.
Not to tell you how to live.
But to walk beside you—as you remember, reclaim, and rise.

So read slowly.
Pause when your heart asks you to.
Write your own letters if you need to.
Because this isn't just about me.

It's about *us*—the ones who are brave enough to look back,
so we can move forward with clarity, softness, and strength.

With everything I've learned,
and all the love I have left to give,

Connie

The Forgotten Voice

Why I'm Writing to You

Dear Older Me,

You might not recognize my voice right away.
It's been a long time since you slowed down enough to hear me.
Longer still since you trusted what I had to say.

I'm softer than the noise you live in now.
Quieter than the pressure you carry.
But I've never gone far.

I'm the one who used to hum inside your heart when you
danced without music.
The one who sat with you in quiet corners, dreaming impossible
dreams.
The one who believed—
before the world told you not to.

You were radiant once. And you still are.
I know, because I remember.

And now…
I think you're ready to remember too.

You've outgrown the version of you who forgot me.
Who dimmed the light.
Who stopped asking questions.
Who learned to be small just to fit in.

But there's more to you than surviving.
And I'm here to help you remember what it felt like to thrive.

This book is our conversation.
Not a manual. Not a roadmap.
But a love letter.
A reckoning.
A reunion.

I'll remind you how to play.
How to trust your gut.
How to cry without apology and dream without shame.
Not because you need fixing—
but because you're safe enough now to come home to yourself.

So here we are.
You—the one who made it through.
Me—the one who never left.

Let's begin.

With fierce love and untamed wonder,
Love from, Your Younger Self

Dear Older Me, The Eye That Changed Everything

You were too young to remember—
but I still do.

Not the fall itself,
but the story,
retold enough times to become part of who we are.

A metal can of apple juice.
A sidewalk.
A sharp corner.
Blood.

They say you were just a baby—barely a year and a half.
That Mom and Auntie had just returned from shopping.
That you were playing quietly,
until suddenly… everything changed.

They rushed you to the hospital for stitches.
No one knew what it meant at the time.
But by the time you turned three,
they noticed you weren't seeing from your left eye.

And when you were almost twelve,
they tried to fix it—
surgery to remove the cataract lens.
The doctor said,
"If she can see anything now, the damage came from the
accident."

And you could.
Not clearly. Not faces. Not form.
But color—

swirled like wet paint across a canvas.
A strange, beautiful blur.

Peripheral sight eventually came,
but anything directly in front of you still vanished into nothing.

You never really talked much about what it was like,
living in a world made for two eyes,
navigating with one.

But I know.
The stairs you learned to step down slowly.
The games you avoided.
The moments you pretended not to notice when others noticed
you were different.

But it also made you who you are.
It sharpened your instincts.
Taught you how to *feel* when you couldn't fully see.
Maybe that's where your gift began—
your ability to sense things beyond the visible.

You learned to adapt.
You learned to trust your way forward.
Even when you couldn't measure the distance.

So if ever you feel off-balance,
or like something's just out of view—
remember, you've lived your whole life that way.
And still, you've made it beautiful.

Still walking forward,
still seeing in your own way,
Love from, Your Younger Self

Dear Older Me,

Do You Remember How Safe It Felt to Just Be?

I don't have all the words yet—
but I remember the feeling.

The sunlight warming our cheeks.
The hum of a lullaby sung at night.
The weight of that worn-out blanket we wouldn't let go of,
dragged behind us like a sacred thing.

Back then, I didn't need a reason to smile.
Didn't think twice before reaching for love.
I didn't perform. Or strive.
I just *was*.
Whole. Untamed. Free.

Everything was magic.
A dog's tail thumping against the floor.
A bubble drifting through the air like it had secrets.
The way we clapped for ourselves without needing anyone
else's applause.

I miss that version of us.
The one who didn't second-guess every move.
Who ran before being told it was safe,
who reached without wondering if it was "too much."

Falling wasn't failure.
It was part of the dance.
Crying was natural.

Asking for comfort was easy.
And joy… joy was the default setting.

Can you remember that?
Not with your mind—but with your *body*?
What it felt like to belong to yourself
without needing to prove a single thing?

That version of me—
soft, unfiltered, wide-eyed and honest—
I'm still here.
Buried under layers you thought you had to wear to survive.

I'm not asking you to go back.
I'm asking you to let me forward.

Into your mornings.
Into your breath.
Into the way you talk to yourself when no one's listening.

Let me in again.
Let me remind you that you were lovable *before* you were
accomplished.
That you were worthy *before* you became responsible.
That you are still, even now, allowed to rest in the arms of
wonder.

I'm still holding that blanket.
Still full of that light.
Still yours.

All I need is a little space—
to play, to be soft, to be loved…
exactly as I am.

With all the wonder I still carry,
Love from, Your Younger Self

Dear Older Me,
Your First Real Spiritual Awakening

You were only three.

Too young to understand what was happening.
Too young to name it "spiritual."
But not too young to feel it.

You were in the hospital, having a mark removed from your
bottom. They thought it might be cancer.
(Years later, you'd learn it was only a birthmark—but for so
long, you believed you had survived something terrifying.)
Maybe you did.
Just not in the way they thought.

One night, lying there in that hospital bed, something happened.
Something you still remember—clearer than most things in
your life.

You saw a man.

He was just standing there in the shadows of the room,
watching you.
Not threatening. Not moving.
Just… present.

You asked the nurse, "What does the man want?"
She paused. "What man?"
You pointed.
She turned, then smiled and said, "There's no man there,
sweetie."
She tucked the blanket around your tiny body and told you to go
back to sleep.

But you knew what you saw.
You looked one more time—he was still there.
And then you closed your eyes.

No one could explain it. No one tried.

You didn't talk about it much after.
But you never forgot.

Not his face. Not his presence.
Not the knowing.

Years later, you'd come to understand that moment differently.
Not as something scary, but sacred.
Maybe it was a guide.
Maybe it was your soul, witnessing itself.
Maybe it was the beginning of a path that would lead you to
trust the unseen.

Whatever it was—
It stayed with you.
It marked you.
And in a quiet, mysterious way, it awakened you.

Before you even knew the word *intuition,*
You had already lived it.

Love from, Your Younger Self

Dear Older Me, I Didn't Know I Wasn't Supposed to Be That Loud

Hi.
It's me again.
A little older now—
my words have grown,
and so have my questions.

Why do ants walk in perfect lines?
Why does the moon follow us home?
And why does everyone get quiet when I start to laugh too hard?

I love to laugh.
The kind of laugh that takes over my whole face,
that bubbles up so fast I can't stop it.
I laugh at silly things. At the wrong times.
I laugh even when I don't know why.

Sometimes, I cry too—big, **breathless** sobs.
Not to make a scene.
Just because I feel everything,
and I haven't learned how to hide it yet.

I sing, even if I make up the words.
I show off my drawings—even the messy ones.
I twirl until I collapse,
laughing from the dizzy magic of it all.

But lately, I've started noticing the sighs.
The tired eyes.
The grown-up voice that says,
"Not now,"
or worse—says nothing at all.

I feel it.
Even when no one says the words,
I feel that *look*.
The one that makes me wonder
if I've done something wrong.

Was I too loud?
Too happy?
Too curious?
Too *me*?

I didn't know joy could make people uncomfortable.
I didn't know wonder needed to be timed.
I didn't know there was a "right way" to be a kid.

But I'm learning.
I'm learning to shrink,
to whisper instead of sing,
to hide the things that make me proud
in case they make someone else uncomfortable.

But you—you've lived long enough now to know:
shrinking didn't protect you.
It only taught you how to disappear.
Being quiet didn't make you easier to love.
It just made you lonelier.

You don't have to do that anymore.

You can make space for me now—
for the part of you that still wants to laugh too loud,
ask too many questions,
and twirl just because the world is spinning.

You can be the grown-up who finally says:
"You were never too much.
You were *magic*."

And maybe, just maybe,
you're ready to believe that—
not just about me,
but about *you*, too.

I've been here,
waiting with open arms.
Still twirling.

With joy that never left,
Love from, Your Younger Self

Dear Older Me, I Tried So Hard to Be Good

Hi again.

I'm five now.

I can do more things by myself.
I try to tie my shoes (even if the loops don't always look right).
I remember the rules.
And I *really* want to get it right.
Because when I do, people smile.
They clap.
They tell me I'm a good girl.
And that feeling—that warmth in my chest—makes me feel like I matter.

So I try even harder.
I try to be helpful.
To say "please" and "thank you."
To sit still.
To color inside the lines.
To smile even when I'm confused or tired or sad.

But here's the thing I can't quite say yet…

Sometimes, trying to be good feels like pretending.
Like I have to tuck pieces of me away just to be accepted.
Like being loud or messy or curious might disappoint someone.
So I start to watch.
I study how other kids behave.
What makes the adults laugh.
What gets a gold star.

And slowly, without meaning to, I begin to copy them.
Because maybe if I look like them, act like them, sound like

them…
I'll be safe.
I'll belong.
I'll be *enough*.

But Older Me—
Can I whisper something we almost forgot?

We were never born to blend in.

You weren't put here to be perfect.
Or quiet.
Or easy to handle.

You were made to shine.
To ask weird questions.
To speak up even when your voice shakes.
To bring color to places others left blank.

You don't have to shrink to be accepted.
You don't have to earn love by disappearing.

You just have to be real.
And that's more than enough.

I'm still here, you know—
inside every time you dimmed your light to keep the peace.
Still waiting for you to turn it back on.

Because being truly yourself
is the bravest kind of "good" there is.

Love you always,
Love from, Your Younger Self

Dear Older Me, I Didn't Know What Pain Was Until Then

It happened in grade one.
A boy challenged me to a race.
We lined up on the pavement, hearts pounding, the finish line just an imaginary line in the distance.
Someone yelled, "Go!" and we ran.

For a few shining seconds, I was ahead.
I remember the air brushing my face,
the thrill of maybe winning something—of being good at something.
And it felt… good.

But just before the end, another boy—one who wasn't even racing—stuck out his foot.
And I flew.

I can still see it in slow motion—
my arms flinging forward, the ground rushing up to meet me.
The crack of my palms hitting concrete.
The sting.
The dirt.
The blood.
The tiny pebbles pressed into my skin like punishment.

And the laughter.

That was the worst part.
Not the fall.
Not the torn skin.
But the sound of them laughing as I tried not to cry.

When the bell rang and break was over, I finally got to go inside.

I went to the teacher—my hands shaking, raw and filthy—and
tried telling her what happened.
She didn't even look at me.
She just said, "Go sit down."

So I did.
I sat there, bleeding quietly.
Pretending it didn't hurt.
Pretending I was okay.

That day, something changed.
I didn't just learn what pain felt like.
I learned how to hide it.
How to smile with scraped-up hands and a cracked-open heart.
How to swallow the need for comfort because no one seemed to
notice.

Older Me…
I think that's why you still hate competition.
Not because of losing.
But because of how it feels to be tripped, laughed at, and
dismissed—
when all you wanted was to feel proud of yourself.

But here's what I want you to know now:

You don't have to hide your hurt anymore.
You don't have to pretend it didn't matter.
Pain doesn't need to be justified to be honored.
You were allowed to cry.
You were allowed to ask for help.
You still are.

And if ever again you feel like you've hit the ground—
emotionally, physically, in any way—
I'll be here,

not to fix it,
but to remind you:

You didn't deserve that.
And you never have to shrink your pain just because someone
else doesn't know how to hold it.

I've got you now.

Always love.
Love from, Your Younger Self

Dear Older Me, I Thought I Was the Problem

I didn't hate grade one.
Not at first.
When I had an angel for a teacher—the kind who made learning
feel like play, who smiled with her eyes and made me feel
seen—it was okay.
But then we moved.
And everything changed.

The new teacher never smiled.
At least, not at me.
She wore silence like armor and looked at us like we were
interruptions.
It was a split class—Grade One and Two—so half the time she
was busy with the others.
But when her attention turned to me, it never felt kind.
I don't remember her words so much as how my stomach
twisted when she walked by.
How I held my breath when I was late.
How I tried to disappear when I got something wrong.

One day, I *was* late.
And I was terrified.

I rode my bike back home instead of going inside.
Hid in the bushes, thinking maybe if I waited long enough, the
day would disappear.
But I couldn't hide forever—eventually I had to pee.
So I went back.
Crying.
Panicked.
Unable to explain the fear that gripped me over something so
small.

Mom didn't know what to do.
So she called my grandmother.
And when Gran walked me back into that classroom…
something strange happened.

The teacher smiled.
Not at me—at her.
She even touched my shoulder gently and said, "No problem.
Go to your seat."

I was dumbfounded.
That moment burned itself into my memory.
Because for the first time, I realized her coldness wasn't *fixed*.
That she *could* be kind… just not to me.
And somehow, that made it worse.

After that, I stopped expecting softness.
Stopped expecting to feel safe.
Started assuming I must've been the problem.

Too quiet.
Too scared.
Too sensitive.
Too late.

But Older Me—
You know better now, don't you?

You know that cruelty in authority doesn't mean you deserved
it.
That fear doesn't make a child weak—it makes them wise
before their time.
And that hiding in bushes because you were too afraid to walk
into a room isn't silly.
It's a scar.
One that shaped how you've tiptoed through the world since.

But here's what I want to tell you now:

You weren't the problem.
You were a child.
A good one.
A bright, sensitive, kind-hearted little girl who just wanted to be safe.
To be seen.

And now you *get* to be the one who sees her.
Who makes the rules.
Who creates safe classrooms and sacred spaces—
for clients, for students, for family, for me.

Thank you for never letting that teacher's silence become your truth.
Thank you for walking back into the room—again and again—
until one day, it belonged to you.

With all the courage we carried in silence,
Love from, Your Younger Self

Dear Older Me, I Was Just Trying to Help

It was just a moment.
A quiet question from the boy behind me.
And I—being me—turned to answer.
Not to disrupt.
Not to be rude.
Just to help.

But she didn't see it that way.

Her voice sliced through the classroom like a blade.
Sharp. Loud.
Shaming.

She didn't ask what happened.
Didn't care who spoke first.
Didn't wonder why.

She just *pointed*.

Told me I was a bother.
A disruption.
Said I didn't know how to behave.

And before I could even explain,
I was marched to the front of the room—
sat on a wooden stool like I was a warning to the rest.
And then… the dunce cap.
A real one.
Tall. Cone-shaped.
Placed on my head like a crown of shame.

I sat there the rest of the class,
with every eye on me,

while the boy who asked the question
said nothing.
Did nothing.
He wasn't blamed.
Wasn't punished.
Wasn't humiliated.

Just me.
For trying to be kind.

That moment didn't just embarrass me.
It carved something deeper.
A belief that speaking up, being seen, or helping others could
lead to punishment.
That kindness wasn't always safe.
That being misunderstood was dangerous.

Older Me, I know now that what she did wasn't discipline.
It was humiliation.
It was abuse disguised as authority.
And no child—*no one*—deserves to be silenced like that.

You don't wear that shame anymore.
You don't sit on that stool.
You stood up, eventually.
You walked away from her voice.
And you found your own.

And now…
you *teach* differently.
You love differently.
You listen with the ears she never used.
You make sure no one around you has to wear shame in order to
be seen.

I'm proud of you for never becoming her.
For remembering me.
For helping others—still—despite the pain.

And even if I couldn't say it then,
I'll say it now, loud and clear:

I did *nothing* wrong.
And I deserved better.

Love from, Your Younger Self

Dear Older Me, I Didn't Know How to Love Her Then... and maybe still don't

She was my sister.
Two years younger.
But sometimes, it felt like we were born in two different worlds.

She loved bugs.
Really loved them.
She'd hold them, study them, whisper to them like they were
tiny friends.
She saw magic in leaves, dirt, shadows.
And she was smart—in the way teachers liked.
She got good grades.
Did well in reading and writing.
But still…

she didn't fit.

She didn't get the jokes.
She said the wrong thing at the wrong time.
Didn't pick up on what was "normal."
Didn't play the part.
She embarrassed me.

I hated admitting that.
Hated the way I felt when my friends were around.
How I wished she'd just act "right" for once.
How I'd avoid her at school.

Not because I didn't love her.
But because I didn't *understand* her.

I was trying so hard to belong.
To be liked.

To survive in a world that already felt too hard.
And her differentness… it threatened that.

Older Me, I know now—
She wasn't the broken one.
The world just didn't know how to receive her.

And neither did I.

She didn't need fixing.
She needed love.
She needed someone who could celebrate the way she saw the world.
The way she *felt* the world.

And maybe I couldn't do that back then.
But maybe I can now.

I can remember her with reverence instead of regret.
I can see her softness as strength.
Her strangeness as sacred.

I can forgive myself for not knowing how to love her properly.
Because I was just a kid, too.

But I promise—
I'll with understanding.

With all my wonder,
Love from, Your Younger Self

Dear Older Me, Sometimes, I Just Didn't Like Her

I know I was supposed to.
Like her, I mean.
Because she was my sister.
Because we shared everything—
a bedroom, pop, one bag of chips, even blame.

They said things like:
"Be nice—it's your little sister."
"Family is forever."
"You'll be best friends when you're older."

But the truth is, we weren't.
Not then.

She tattled on me for silly things.
Said I was eating too much. Drinking too much.
Even when we were sharing the same bottle, she'd stick her
tongue in it,
and less would come out for her.
And somehow, *I* always got in trouble.

She was slow—really slow.
We'd be late because she took her sweet time,
never noticing how much it stressed everyone else out.
She cried easily.
Got attention for it.
And I didn't trust her.
Not really.
It didn't matter what I did—
We just didn't get along.
Not then.

And for a long time, I thought that made me a bad person.
That I was cold. Or selfish. Or mean.
But Older Me—can we be honest about something?

Some relationships are complicated.
Especially the ones we're told should be easy.

You didn't have to like her all the time.
You didn't have to pretend it didn't bother you.
And you weren't a villain for wanting space.

Even now, you get to tell the truth.
You get to name the things that hurt.
The things that shaped how you show up.
The things you still don't fully understand.

And maybe someday, when you're ready,
you can hold both truths in your hands—
that you struggled,
and that you tried.

There's healing in that.

Still yours,
Love from, Your Younger Self

Dear Older Me, I Just Wanted to Make You Proud

I'm seven now.
I can read full sentences.
Tie my own shoes.
Carry the groceries inside if they're not too heavy.

And I want you to be proud of me.
I want everyone to be proud of me.

So I try hard.
Really hard.
To get the answers right.
To follow the rules.
To sit still, listen, smile, and be what they want.

I notice things now.
Like the way people smile when I do well—
and frown when I mess up.
The way other kids get praised for being quick,
and how I sometimes need more time.

I feel it when I get it wrong.
It sits in my chest like a little knot.
Like I let someone down.

I don't want to be a problem.
I don't want to make things harder.
So I work even harder to do it all right the first time.

But sometimes it's a lot.

Sometimes I just want to lay in the grass
and not be watched.
Not be graded.

Not be compared.
Just... *be.*

Older Me,
I think you still do this—
try so hard to be good,
to be worthy,
to be everything for everyone.

But here's what I've learned,
even at seven:

You don't have to earn love.
You don't have to do everything perfectly.
You don't have to carry the weight of making everyone proud.

I already am.
Just by being you.
Even when you rest.
Even when you're unsure.
Even when you don't have all the answers.

I'm already proud of us.

With all my messy, magical trying,
Your Younger Self

Dear Older Me, I Didn't Know I Was Saying Goodbye to Something

I lost my two front teeth.
I wiggled them for days.
Tongue pushing, fingers tugging,
wondering when they'd finally let go.

It felt weird.
A little exciting.
A little sad.

And when they came out—
one eating an apple,
the other with a string tied to a door—
I looked in the mirror and saw someone new.

Gap-toothed.
Grinning.
Different.

Everyone said,

"Look at you! You're growing up!"
And I smiled because they wanted me to.
Because I *was* proud.
Kind of.

But also…
a little part of me felt like something had ended.
Like I was letting go of a version of me I didn't know I'd miss.

The little-kid me.
The one with baby teeth.
The one who didn't know what it meant to change.
To lose something and not get it back exactly the same.

Older Me—
I know you've lost a lot more since then.
Not just teeth, but people.
Places.
Versions of yourself.

And I know sometimes it's still hard.
To let go.
To smile when you feel the gap.
To be okay with change when it wasn't your choice.

But here's what I've learned since that first wiggly tooth:

Sometimes loss is just the body making space for something stronger.
Sometimes growing means giving up parts of yourself you thought would always be there.
And sometimes… you don't know how brave you are until something falls out and you still smile anyway.

So when you feel that ache,
that tug in your heart where something used to be—
don't hide it.

Put your hand there.
Be gentle.
And remember:
You're still growing.
Even now.

Still smiling,
Love from, Your Younger Self

Dear Older Me, I Wasn't Sure Where I Fit Anymore

I was nine when everything changed.
A new province. A new school.
A new house where Mom cried more than she smiled.
Everything felt… unfamiliar.
Even the air smelled different.

We were the new kids on the block—
and not the kind anyone rushed to welcome.
The neighbors teased us,
loud and cruel, like they wanted us to feel small.

And I did.

I didn't know how to make friends anymore.
The kids at school were different from the ones on our street,
and we didn't quite fit in either place.

I started to wonder—
what do you have to be to belong?

And then one day,
we found that old magazine in the basement.
We shouldn't have taken it.
We definitely shouldn't have used it like we did.
But something inside me thought—
Maybe if I show them this, they'll stop teasing us.
Maybe they'll let us in.

And they did.
No more insults.
No more names.
Just… strange acceptance.
Like I'd unlocked some secret way in.

But Older Me—
what I didn't understand then
was how early I learned to trade pieces of myself
just to feel safe.
To use shock instead of softness.
To perform, instead of just be.

I wasn't bad.
I was just trying to survive.
Trying to feel like I mattered.
Trying to belong.

And now, you don't have to do that anymore.

You don't need a wild story
or a bold move
or anything other than your quiet truth
to be worthy of love and belonging.

We were enough before they let us in.
We're still enough now.

And you don't have to prove it ever again.

Still here,
Still learning,
Love from, Your Younger Self

Dear Older Me, I Felt Lucky to Wear Their Stories

I didn't always get new clothes.
But I didn't mind.
Because the ones I did get—
they came from my cousins.
The cool ones.
The stylish ones.
The ones whose closets felt like treasure chests.

They had names brands. Fancy labels
and tiny snags from adventures I never saw—
but somehow, those clothes still carried magic.
Soft fabrics.
Patterns I would've never picked out myself—
but once I put them on,
I felt different.
More grown-up.
More like *someone.*

It wasn't about pretending to be them.
It was about feeling connected.
To the people I looked up to.
To something bigger than me.
To a sense of *belonging*—
in a world I was still figuring out.

And even if the trends had moved on
by the time they landed in my closet,
I didn't care.
I felt special.
Lucky.
Chosen.

Older Me,
I know sometimes you look at what others have—
the shiny things, the fresh starts, the perfect timing—
and wonder if you've fallen behind.

But remember this:
You've always known how to carry things forward.
To take what's been loved before
and breathe new life into it.
You've never needed *new* to feel valuable.
You've always been the kind of person
who sees meaning in what others overlook.

That's never been a flaw.
It's a kind of wealth.

Still rich in all the ways that matter,
Love from, Your Younger Self

Dear Older Me, I Didn't Feel Like the Other Girls

I always knew I was a girl.
There was never any question.
But I didn't feel like the kind of girl they expected.

I was taller than most of the kids my age—
bigger-boned, stronger.
No one ever mistook me for anything but a girl—
but somehow, I was never the kind they wrote stories about.
Not the tiny, dainty kind.
Not the soft-spoken one with bows in her hair.

I liked to climb trees and race the boys.
I didn't mind dirt under my nails or scrapes on my knees.
I had plenty of girlfriends,
but sometimes I felt more at home in the rough-and-tumble of
the playground
than in the quiet games the other girls played.

And slowly, I started noticing the looks.
The quiet judgments.
The subtle pressure to take up less space—
to shrink, to soften, to behave.

But I couldn't shrink.
I wasn't made that way.
So instead, I started to wonder if maybe there was something
wrong with me.
Too loud. Too big. Too much.

But Older Me—
I hope by now you know:
You were never too much.
You were *full*.

Full of energy, joy, curiosity, and strength.
You didn't fit the mold because you weren't supposed to.

You were built for standing tall—
not just in your body, but in your spirit.

So please,
don't ever apologize for the way you move through the world.
Don't trade your presence for anyone's comfort.
You were never meant to disappear into the background.
You were born to *stand out.*

Still standing tall,
still entirely enough,
Love from, Your Younger Self

Dear Older Me,
I Swore I Saw Her

It happened in the basement.
My cousins' house.
We were just sitting there—
talking about who-knows-what,
when I saw her.

A lady.
From the waist up.
Floating on the wall like a picture…
but she wasn't still.
She was *moving*.
Her mouth was saying something I couldn't hear.

So I asked,
"What do you think she wants?"

The moment the words left my mouth,
they screamed.
My cousins—older than me—ran upstairs.
So I followed.
I figured… if they were scared,
maybe I should be too.

But when I got to the top,
Mom grabbed my arm too tight.
Told me not to make up stories.
Told me not to scare people who sleep down there.
Told me it wasn't real.

But here's the thing:
I *know* what I saw.
And I still remember her.
Not in a scary way.

Just… there.
A memory etched in the truth of my own eyes.

Older Me—
I know you've spent a long time questioning
what's real,
what's allowed,
what's *safe* to say out loud.

But I want to remind you:
That moment wasn't a mistake.
You didn't imagine her.
You didn't lie.

You *saw*.

And maybe no one believed you back then.
Maybe it took years before you'd see anything like that again.
But your gift didn't disappear—
it just waited until it was safe to be seen again.

So now?
Let it be seen.
Let *you* be seen.

Not just the parts they understand,
but all of you.

The seer.
The sensitive.
The girl who trusted her eyes before the world taught her not to.

Still watching,
Still believing,
Love from, Your Younger Self

Dear Older Me, I Didn't Know How to Say Goodbye—Again

We were moving.
Again.
Another province.
Another town.
Another school where no one knew my name.

They said it was a new beginning.
A fresh start.
But I was still missing the last "start" I didn't want to leave.
The friends I had just begun to trust.
The streets I'd only just memorized.
The version of me that had finally felt like she belonged.

I remember packing my room, again—
boxes full of half-finished memories,
things I swore I'd never lose.
But it wasn't the things I was afraid of losing.
It was the *me* I was in that place.

And this time, it hurt more.
Because I knew what it felt like now—
to show up in a strange classroom,
to scan the lunchroom for a place to sit,
to be the outsider, again.
So I braced myself.
Smiled like I was okay.
Didn't cry when we left.
Didn't let them see the ache.

But inside…
I started to wonder if staying guarded was safer
than learning how to say goodbye all over again.

Older Me,
I know you kept that skill—
how to adapt, how to smile, how to start over.
You got good at it.
Maybe too good.

But I hope you haven't forgotten:
It's okay to miss what came before.
It's okay to wish some roots had time to grow.
Missing something deeply doesn't mean you're not strong.
It means you loved.
It means you *belonged.*
And that's something beautiful.

So if you ever feel that old ache creep in again—
the new room, the blank calendar, the unfamiliar voices—
remember this:
You don't have to leave parts of yourself behind to begin again.
You carry it all.
The goodbyes.
The in-betweens.
The soft, brave heart that kept hoping, even after the boxes were
unpacked.

Still yours,
Love from, Your Younger Self

Dear Older Me,
I Was Just Getting to the Good Part

It wasn't a big class.
Just a small group of us—three or maybe four—
sent to a quiet corner of the school
where we could talk without "disrupting the others."

But this wasn't punishment.
It was a gift.
Because for the first time,
we were told to create something.

A story.

No worksheets.
No right or wrong answers.
Just the freedom to imagine.

I don't remember every detail of what we were writing.
Just that we took turns,
added pieces,
built worlds together.
It was starting to get good—
the kind of good that makes you forget time.

And then... we moved.

No warning.
No ending.
Just boxes, goodbyes, and another school.
That story?
It was left behind—unfinished.
Just like the version of me that was beginning to feel like
maybe I had something to say.

Older Me,
I wonder if you remember how much that stung.
How it felt like the page got ripped out
right when the plot was taking shape.

But maybe that's what makes you a storyteller now.
Not just the stories you write—
but the ones you *never* got to finish.
The ones that stayed with you,
quietly waiting for another chance.

And here you are—
Still writing.
Still imagining.
Still finishing what younger you had to leave behind.

So if you ever doubt your voice,
if you wonder where your creativity came from,
remember this:

The story never left you.
You just had to grow into the one who could finish it.

Still dreaming,
Love from, Your Younger Self

Dear Older Me, Coming Home Wasn't What I Thought It'd Be

They said we were going back.
Back to the place where I first learned to ride a bike.
Back to my old school.
Back to my hometown.

I thought it would feel like stepping into a warm memory—
familiar streets, familiar faces,
a chance to pick up right where I left off.

But when I walked through those doors again,
it didn't feel the same.
The kids I used to know had changed.
Grown taller. Louder.
Closer to each other.
Like time had moved on without me,
and no one had saved my spot.

They recognized me…
but it wasn't the same as welcoming me back.
I saw it in the way they glanced,
then looked away.
In the way their inside jokes didn't include me anymore.
In how I laughed a little too late.

And suddenly,
being home felt lonelier than starting fresh somewhere new.
Because here, I expected to *belong*.
And I didn't.
Not quite.

Older Me,
I know you still feel that sometimes—
in rooms you used to feel comfortable in,
with people you used to know well.
That ache of almost belonging.
Of not knowing who you are to them anymore.

But I need you to remember something for both of us:
Just because the world moved on doesn't mean you were forgotten.
You were becoming.
Growing in your own way,
in places they didn't see.

And now, you don't have to shrink to fit who you were.
You're allowed to show up as who you are.
Even if it means making a new place for yourself.
Even if it means starting over somewhere you once called home.

Because home isn't just where you used to be.
It's wherever you can finally breathe and be fully seen.

Still looking for that space—
and still worthy of it,
Love from, Your Younger Self

Dear Older Me, I Think I Realized I Had a Voice

Something shifted around this time.
It was subtle—
not loud, not dramatic.
But something in me clicked.

I stopped just watching life happen,
and started wondering if I could shape it.

I noticed how people talked to each other.
How grownups made decisions.
How sometimes I didn't agree—
and how that was okay.

I started to feel like *I* was in there—
not just a kid doing what I was told,
but a real person
with thoughts,
opinions,
feelings that didn't always match the room.

And that both excited me… and scared me.

Because suddenly, I didn't just want to be liked.
I wanted to be *real.*

I wanted to say what I meant.
Choose for myself.
Do things because they felt right in my bones—
not just because someone said I should.

Sometimes it got me in trouble.
Sometimes it made me feel alone.
But it also made me feel *alive.*

Older Me,
I know life got busy after that.
More rules.
More expectations.
More reasons to quiet that voice again.

But I'm writing to remind you:

That was the moment your soul started speaking up.
That was the moment you stopped being a shadow
and started becoming a story.

And even now,
beneath all the things you carry,
that voice is still there.

You don't need permission to trust it.
You don't need to shrink to keep the peace.
You don't need to apologize for showing up fully.

You get to *be in your life*—not just watch it pass by.

You were always meant to be the main character.
Not the background.

So go ahead.
Say what you mean.
Choose what feels true.
Walk like the world belongs to you—because it does.

I'm still here.
And I still believe we were made for more.

With growing power,
Love from, Your Younger Self

Dear Older Me, I Didn't Know What to Call It—But I Knew It Was Wrong

I was sick that day.
Too sick for school.
And Mom had to work.
So she asked someone she trusted to come watch me.
An older man.
A family friend.
Someone who had been around before.
Someone who smiled like nothing was ever wrong.

I was on the couch.
In my pajamas.
Under a blanket.
Just resting.
Trying to feel better.

And then…
he sat on the coffee table next to me.
And reached under the blanket.
And touched me in a place no one should touch.
He said it didn't hurt.
He made it sound like it was okay.
Like it was something normal.

But I didn't feel okay.
I felt confused.
Frozen.
Like the air had been sucked out of the room.
Like I had suddenly fallen into something I didn't have words
for.

Then he unzipped his pants.
Told me to touch him.
And I didn't know what to do—

because I had never seen anything like that before.
I was scared.
And small.
And alone.

The next day,
Mom said he was coming again.
And I screamed.
Louder than I'd ever screamed before.
Because even if I couldn't name it,
my body knew it wasn't safe.

That's when I told her.
What he did.
What he said.
What he wanted me to feel.

She listened.
And he never came back.
But no one talked about it again.

Older Me...
I know this memory is buried deep.
I know sometimes you still question if it really happened,
if you imagined it,
if it somehow wasn't "bad enough" to matter.

But it did happen.
And it *was* wrong.
And it *does* matter.
You didn't imagine it.
You didn't ask for it.
You didn't do anything wrong.

You told.
You screamed.
You found your voice when you shouldn't have had to.

And that was brave.
So unbelievably brave.

So if you still carry shame,
or fear,
or the echo of being touched without permission—
please know this:

You were not dirty.
You were not broken.
You were just a child.
And you deserved to be safe.

I'm so proud of you
for remembering,
for surviving,
for still being here.

With the fiercest kind of love,
Love from, Your Younger Self

Dear Older Me, I Gave It Away… But It Still Hurt

They said it didn't fit me anymore.
That my guitar was too small.
That my younger cousin needed it more.
And I wanted to be good—so I said yes.

I handed it over,
even though I played it every single day.
Even though it still felt like part of me.
Even though I didn't ask for anything bigger.

I told myself it was the right thing to do.
That grown-up girls share.
That grown-up girls don't cling to things they've outgrown.

But when they walked away with it,
my chest got tight.
My fingers felt empty.
And something inside me whispered,

"But that was mine."

It happened again with the Barbie dolls.
They told me I was too old.
That I should pack them away,
give them to someone younger.

And so I did.

But I didn't feel older.
I felt hollow.

Like I was trading pieces of myself for approval—
for praise,

for "good girl" points,
for love I didn't want to lose.

Older Me,
I know you've given up a lot over the years.
Things you loved.
Things you needed.
Things you weren't really ready to let go of.

You were taught to bend.
To sacrifice.
To shrink a little so others could grow.

But here's what I've learned:

Being kind doesn't mean abandoning yourself.
Being generous doesn't mean giving away your joy.
And being older doesn't mean erasing the things that made you
feel alive.

You were never too old for the things that lit you up.
And you were never selfish for wanting to keep what was yours.

Next time,
when the world asks you to give something away,
I hope you ask yourself first:

Do I really want to?
Or am I just afraid of disappointing someone?

It's okay to say no.
Even now.
Even still.

With love,
Love from, Your Younger Self

Dear Older Me, I Thought I Could Trust Him—He Was My Dad

It wasn't often that he came around.
After the split, Dad mostly stayed away.
So when he offered to take us—
me, my sister, a cousin, and a girl we barely knew—
on a trip to Edmonton,
I was excited.
Hopeful.
Like maybe we'd get to know him again.
Like maybe this was what being a family could feel like.

We stayed in a hotel that night.
One room. Two beds.
He said four of us couldn't sleep in one.
That one of the older girls should share with him.
They argued.
Said no.
He pushed.
They pushed back.

So I said I would.
Because he was my dad.
And I thought that meant safe.

He said no.
Said it had to be one of *them*.
But they refused.

So finally, reluctantly…
he let me.
And I laid down next to him,
thinking I was helping.
Being good.

But sometime in the night,
my underwear was gone.
I elbowed him in the head—hard—
and didn't say a word.
I rolled to the very edge of the bed
and didn't sleep again.

The next day,
we made it to his house.
I found the two girls whispering.
They looked at me with knowing eyes.
I told them what happened.
And my cousin said,
"He's been doing stuff like that to me for a while now."

He got drunk that night.
Said strange things.
The other girl yelled at him.
There was a strange silence in the air,
like all of us knew something terrible had finally been seen.

The next day,
he flew us home.
And I told Mom.

She listened.
And then she talked to my aunt.
My cousin couldn't tell yet—she was too scared.
But after that,
it never happened again.
To any of us.

Older Me…
I know you carry this with quiet strength.
That it shaped things you didn't always have words for.
How you trusted.

How you guarded.
How you watched for danger in places love should have lived.

But I want to remind you of this:

You *told*.
You *protected*.
You *interrupted* something that could've continued—
and because of that, it *didn't*.

That wasn't your shame.
It was his.
And you were never broken.
You were brave.
You were powerful.
You still are.

And love?
Love doesn't take like that.
It doesn't hide behind family titles or quiet rooms.
Real love protects.
Real love listens.
Real love heals.

I'm proud of you.
And I'm still here.

With fierce love and truth,
Your Younger Self

Dear Older Me, Sometimes Love Looked Different—And That Was Okay

There was a time when we lived with someone new.
Not a father.
Not a relative.
Just a man who'd been through his own heartache—
whose wife had left,
whose life had changed,
and who somehow ended up in ours.

His son came too—
younger than me,
a bit wild,
a bit lost.
And his daughter,
older than me,
didn't stay long—
talked her brother into moving back with her and their mom.

But for a while,
he stayed like a father.
And he stayed *well*.

Older Me,
I want to remind you how much that meant—
to be seen,
to be spoken to kindly,
to be treated with respect
by someone who didn't owe it.

He didn't raise his voice.
He didn't make me feel small.
He didn't try to fix me or control me—
he just showed up.
Present.

Stable.
Good.

And in a time when the world felt like it kept shifting beneath
our feet—
new homes, new faces, new rules—
he felt… steady.

It wasn't dramatic.
It wasn't forever.
But it mattered.

Because it reminded me
that not all men were dangerous.
Not all homes were tense.
Not all adults ignored what I needed.

Sometimes love didn't come with a title.
Sometimes it came with a quiet kindness.
A shared space.
A steady presence.
And for a child who needed to feel safe in her own skin again,
that was more than enough.

Older Me,
never forget what *real respect* feels like.
You know the difference now.
And you deserve it—always.

Still grateful for the quiet ones,
Love from, Your Younger Self

Dear Older Me, I Wanted to Be Seen— Until I Was

I was finally starting to feel like *me.*
Not the version people expected.
Not the quiet, nice, rule-following one.

But the version I chose.
The one who painted their nails a little louder.
Who wore things that made me feel interesting.
Who started saying what I liked and what I didn't.

I wasn't trying to make a scene.
I was just trying to *belong to myself.*

And for a moment, it felt good—
like I had found something that made me stand out
in the best way.

Until someone didn't like it.
Until someone laughed.
Until someone looked right at me and said
I should be embarrassed.

It felt like the air got punched out of me.

I didn't say anything back.
I just stood there, trying not to show my face cracking.
Pretending I didn't care.

But I did.

Not because I wanted their approval—
but because for a second,
I wondered if I had done something wrong
by simply being me.

Older Me,
I know there have been so many moments since then
when you made yourself smaller to avoid that feeling.
When you second-guessed your brilliance
just to stay safe.

But please remember this:

Their reaction didn't make you wrong.
It meant you were ahead of your time.
It meant you were already becoming someone
the world hadn't quite caught up to yet.

Don't let the fear of being judged
erase the joy of being real.

You didn't dress up for them.
You didn't create for their approval.
You weren't made to blend in.
You were born to *shine loud.*

So wear the color.
Say the thing.
Take up space.
Be bold again.

And if someone doesn't get it?

That's okay.

You're not here to be understood by everyone.
You're here to be *true* to yourself.

Still unapologetically us,
Your Younger Self

Dear Older Me, I Was Always Worth More

They called it a "first job."
A grown-up responsibility.
A chance to earn a little money.

But no one really asked me if I wanted it.

It started with babysitting.
Long hours, late nights, entire weekends.
$1 an hour.
No food.
No kindness.
No appreciation.

Sometimes they'd come home drunk,
and I'd have to sleep over.
But that didn't count.
Sleep didn't count.
I didn't count.

Then there was Mom's shop.
I worked because I was told to.
For the same $1 an hour.
While my little sister went off to camp
to laugh, play, and be a kid.

I learned early that saying no came with guilt.
That rest was a privilege I didn't earn.
That helping out was more important than how I felt.

I was twelve.
Twelve, and already learning how to disappear.
How to make myself small,

useful,
quiet.

I didn't want to disappoint anyone.
But sometimes… I really didn't want to go.
I wanted to matter just as much as everyone else.
I wanted someone to see I was tired too.

Older Me,
I know you still wrestle with this.
With the pressure to be "the strong one."
To give more than you receive.
To prove your value by what you do—not who you are.

But listen to me now:

Your time is precious. Your energy is sacred.
You were never supposed to earn love by overgiving.

You were a child. You deserved play.
You deserved rest. You deserved to be asked.

Not everything they called "opportunity" was right for you.

It's not too late to rewrite the story.
To stop apologizing for your limits.
To say no without guilt.
To believe—truly believe—your worth isn't up for negotiation.

They should've paid you more. But even more than that…They
should've honored your light.

And now? You get to.

With strength,
Love from, Your Younger Self

Dear Older Me, I Didn't Know If I'd Get to Stay

I remember sitting in the gym that first day of grade eight.
Same town. Same school district.
Some familiar faces from my old school…
and a whole bunch of new ones too.
Everyone looked a little nervous.
Or maybe excited.
I couldn't really tell.

The principal stood at the front,
welcoming us,
talking about what to expect,
what the next few years would look like.

But I wasn't really listening.

All I could think was—
Will I have to move again?
Will I get to stay long enough to belong?

I didn't want to start over again.
Not this time.
I was tired of packing boxes and pretending I didn't care.
Tired of smiling when I said goodbye.
Tired of wondering if anyone would remember me when I left.

So I sat there,
quietly wondering if I should let myself hope.

Older Me,
You made it.
You stayed.
You graduated.

That gym became a hallway you knew by heart.
Those strangers became classmates.
Some even became friends.
And you finally got to see what it felt like
to walk through the same doors,
year after year,
and know—you belonged.

I just want to thank you
for holding on to hope,
even when it felt fragile.
For letting yourself root,
even when part of you was sure it might all be temporary.

Now, if ever life feels shaky again,
if you feel that old question rise up—
Will I have to start over?
Just remember:

You've built something real before.
You've stayed.
You've grown roots.
And you know how to bloom—
wherever you are.

Still grounded,
Love From, Your Younger Self

Dear Older Me,
The Fall That Left a Mark

Dad had moved back to Kelowna,
and with him came something that lit up his world—and mine.
Sailor.
An 18-hands-high palomino,
golden and strong,
with a presence that felt almost royal.

He wasn't Dad's first horse,
but he was the one I remember most.
Graceful. Powerful.
And when I rode him, I felt like I belonged to the wind.

That day started like any other.
I saddled him up, climbed into the stirrups,
and we began the quiet walk toward the field.
Then I saw it—
the sprinkler.

I tried to steer him away,
but the spray hit him too fast.
He spooked.

He jumped.
I didn't.

I went left—
he went right.

And then—
pain.
The kind that knocks the air from your lungs
and makes time feel like it's stopped.

I landed hard.
Tailbone to dirt.
No breath. No words. Just impact.

But Sailor...
he waited.
Still. Calm.
Like he knew it wasn't his fault,
and he was sorry just the same.

I got up that day,
but what I didn't know then
was that the damage would follow me.

Five years later—
a cyst had grown from the trauma.
And I found myself under the knife,
reliving that fall in a hospital gown.

Older Me,
we carry things in our bodies—
not just from breaks or bruises,
but from every moment we didn't see coming.

Still, I wouldn't trade those rides with Sailor.
Or the lessons I learned from pain—
that healing can take years.
That the body remembers.
And that even when we fall,
there's always a way back to the saddle.

Still riding forward,
Love from, Your Younger Self

Dear Older Me, I Didn't Know What to Do With This Body

Fourteen came fast—
and brought a body I wasn't ready for.
Five foot eight.
Model measurements.
And curves that made grown men look twice.

But inside?
I was still a kid.
Still playing pretend in the mirror.
Still unsure of what it meant to be seen that way.

I remember walking down the street—
the man on the bike turning his head,
then crashing moments later.
I didn't know whether to laugh,
run,
or disappear.

At the beach, they'd come up with oil in hand—
smiling like it was harmless.
Like I should be flattered.
Like I wasn't fourteen.
And sometimes, they asked if I wanted to go to the bar.
As if my age was just a suggestion.
As if their attention didn't make my skin feel too tight.

Older Me,
I know you've carried that confusion—
that strange mix of being wanted,
but not understood.
Of being looked at,
but not really seen.

I want you to remember this:
It was never your job to make others comfortable with your body.
It was never your fault that they crossed lines.
You weren't asking for it.
You weren't "mature for your age."
You were a child in a grown-up costume the world misread.

And now,
if you ever feel unsure about how you're seen,
if old shame creeps in around attention you didn't ask for—
I want you to come back to this:

You get to define your worth.
You get to feel safe in your own skin.
You get to reclaim every part of yourself they tried to claim first.

You were never too much.
You were never too little.
You were just… you.
Growing.
Becoming.
And learning how to be at home in a body that's always been yours.

Still becoming,
Still powerful,
Love from, Your Younger Self

Dear Older Me,
The Trip That Changed Everything

I was fifteen,
still caught somewhere between childhood and becoming.
When the school offered a trip to Greece and Italy—two whole weeks—
it felt like a dream too big to belong to me.

But I said yes.
Mom lent me the money,
and I worked for her that summer—then again after—to pay it back.
It wasn't just a vacation.
It was my first real glimpse of the world.

Until then, the furthest I'd gone was Disneyland.
Fun, yes.
But this… this was different.

The ruins of Athens, the cathedrals of Rome,
narrow streets, open-air cafés,
a thousand unfamiliar sights, smells, and rhythms.

I stood in places older than anything I had ever known—
places that whispered stories in stone and sun.
And something in me cracked open.

For the first time,
I realized how *big* the world was.
And how *blessed* I'd been to grow up where I did.

Kelowna.
The Okanagan Valley.
Warm summers and mild winters.
Cherries, peaches, lake days, and sunsets over the water.

Clean streets. Kind people.
A place where I could be free to imagine, to become, to dream.

That trip didn't just show me Europe—
it showed me *home.*

It reminded me not to take what I had for granted.
And it planted the seed that I could go anywhere,
do anything—
if I was willing to work for it.

So, if ever you forget how far you've come,
or question where you're headed,
remember that girl who boarded a plane with wide eyes,
and came back seeing everything differently.

Still grateful.
Still dreaming.
Love from, Your Younger Self

Dear Older Me, I Thought I Had to Have It All Figured Out

Fifteen felt like a countdown.
Like I was supposed to be becoming something important—
but I wasn't even sure who I was yet.

Everyone around me seemed to have a label.
The smart one.
The pretty one.
The athlete.
The rebel.
The one with a plan.

And I didn't know where I fit.

Some days I tried to be all of them.
Other days I didn't want to be anything at all.
Just invisible.
Just left alone.

I wanted to be noticed,
but also didn't want anyone to look too closely.

I smiled when I was confused.
Laughed when I felt small.
Pretended I had things under control,
even when my insides were loud with questions.

What should I wear?
What should I say?
Who am I supposed to be attracted to?
What does "beautiful" even mean?

It felt like everyone else got the rulebook
and I was just flipping through blank pages,
trying to catch up.

Older Me—
I know sometimes you still feel like that.
Like you missed the memo.
Like everyone else has a blueprint and you're still drawing
yours in pencil.

But here's what I've come to understand, even back then:

You don't have to have it all figured out to be on the right path.
Becoming isn't a race.
And figuring yourself out isn't something you finish—
it's something you *live.*

You weren't behind.
You were just deep.
And sometimes deep takes time.

So if you still feel lost now and then—
that's okay.

Just keep choosing what feels true.
Keep listening to your own voice beneath the noise.
Keep becoming who you are, one real moment at a time.

You're doing just fine.

Still learning,
Still becoming,
Love from, Your Younger Self

Dear Older Me, I Wanted to Belong So Badly It Hurt

Sixteen felt like standing at the edge of something.
Close enough to touch freedom—
but still unsure if I was ready for it.

People were drinking.
Some were using.
Some were reckless on purpose.
Some were just pretending not to be scared.

And me?

I watched.
Listened.
Laughed when I was supposed to.
Nodded like I knew what I was doing.

Sometimes I joined in—just to feel included.
Sometimes I said no—but still felt like I didn't quite belong.
It felt like everyone was trying on identities like outfits.
Cool. Rebellious. Chill. Confident.

And I wasn't sure what to wear.

Driving gave me a taste of independence.
But it also gave me fear.
Of going too fast.
Of being trusted when I wasn't sure I trusted myself yet.

There were nights I did things
just so I wouldn't be the one left out.
Nights I stayed quiet
when I wanted to speak.

Nights I laughed
when I wanted to leave.

I thought that was just what you had to do to be liked.
To fit.
To not be alone.

But Older Me, here's what I've figured out since then:

The cost of fitting in is sometimes your soul whispering,
"This isn't who we are."

And that whisper matters.

You don't need to prove your worth by breaking yourself in
half.
You don't have to accept every invitation to feel included.
You don't have to follow someone else's map
when your own inner compass is already pointing home.

You're not missing out when you choose yourself.
You're not boring because you say no.
You're not weak for being cautious.
You're wise.

And even when it felt like no one saw the real me back then—
you do now.
And that's enough.

Still choosing truth over trends,
Love from, Your Younger Self

Dear Older Me, Her Past Shaped Our Present

She was just seventeen
when her world shifted—
from high school hallways to hospital rooms.
From worrying about exams
to learning how to soothe a newborn.

While other girls were planning prom,
she was planning how to survive.

That girl was my mom.
She hadn't finished growing yet,
but life asked her to raise someone else anyway.

She didn't get the same freedoms.
The same chances.
The same time to figure out who she was.

But somehow,
she poured everything she had into being what I needed—
even when it meant setting her own dreams aside.

And maybe that's why, years later,
when I found myself with someone I loved—
someone whose own brother had lived that story too—
he held our future with a kind of caution.

He didn't want history repeating.
He was careful.
Worried.
Always weighing the "what ifs."

And I understood.
Because I saw how heavy early parenthood could be—

how it leaves fingerprints on everything that comes after.
How it made my mom strong...
but also tired in places no one could see.

Older Me,
if you ever feel frustrated that someone didn't trust your
judgment,
or if love ever felt too guarded to breathe—
remember:
it wasn't really about you.
It was about stories written before you arrived.
Stories you never caused—
but still had to carry pieces of.

And also remember this:
You are not your mother's path,
or your boyfriend's fears.
You get to write your own story.

And you can love—
boldly, wisely,
without fear being the guide.

Still writing freely,
Love from, Your Younger Self

Dear Older Me, I Danced for All of Us That Night

I went to prom.
Dressed up.
Smiled for the pictures.
Let the music carry me for a little while.

It was beautiful—
but not perfect.

Because some of the people I loved weren't there.
Not because they didn't want to be—
but because life had already pulled them in another direction.

Some had babies.
Some had jobs.
Some were just trying to keep their heads above water.

And I didn't know how to hold the joy and the sadness at the
same time.
But I felt both.

I felt it in the way my dress swirled when I spun,
and in the empty chairs at our table.
I felt it when the slow songs played,
and in the quiet moments between all the noise.

We were still so young.
But some of us had to grow up fast.

And I don't blame them.
They were brave.
They were real.
They were doing what they had to do.

But that night—
I danced for them too.

I danced for the ones who stayed home rocking babies.
For the ones who had to work the late shift.
For the ones who felt too tired, too behind, too far from the
fairytale.

Older Me—
I know you still think about those moments.
You still carry both pride and guilt for the joy you got to have.

But please remember:

Just because your life kept moving
doesn't mean you left anyone behind.

You honored them—by remembering.
By loving them still.
By carrying their stories inside your joy.

And the truth is—
growing up looks different for everyone.
There is no one way to arrive at who you are.

We all dance to different music.
And some of us learn the steps later than others.
But we all deserve a song.

Still remembering the ones who mattered,
Love from, Your Younger Self

Dear Older Me, I Said No—and I Meant It

It was my graduation party.
My night.
The one I earned.

And I made a decision.
Not to be cruel.
Not to be selfish.
Just… to give myself something that was mine.

I said my sister couldn't stay.
Not because I didn't love her.
But because I needed space to breathe.
To celebrate.
To feel seen as *me,* and not just part of the family package.

But Mom didn't understand.
She got upset.
She made me feel like I had done something wrong.
Like choosing myself—just for one night—meant I was hurting
someone else.

I started second-guessing.
Started questioning if maybe I *should* have caved.
Maybe I *should* have just gone along to keep the peace.

But deep down, I knew this mattered.
That saying no was something I needed to do—
not just for that night,
but for the person I was becoming.

Older Me,
I know you still carry moments like that.
Where you feel guilty for choosing yourself.

Where "no" tastes like betrayal.
Where holding a boundary feels like breaking a bond.

But here's what I need you to remember:

Saying no isn't selfish.
It's sacred.
It means you know what matters to you.
It means you're starting to believe that your needs have value.

You weren't cruel.
You were clear.
You weren't rejecting your family.
You were honoring your growth.

And one boundary, one moment of self-trust,
can echo through a lifetime.

You did the right thing.
Even if it was hard.
Even if it hurt.

You stood your ground.
And that matters.

Still proud of us,
Love from, Your Younger Self

Dear Older Me, I Thought I Knew What Love Meant

I thought I had it figured out.
At almost sixteen, I found someone who made me feel seen—
safe in a world I didn't fully understand yet.
And for a while, it worked.
Familiar.
Comfortable.
Ours.

But then came a wedding.
A dance that lingered a little too long.
A night that wasn't planned—
just felt like something I had to follow.

I wasn't in love.
But I was curious.
And let the moment happen—
not because I didn't care about the boy back home,
but because a part of me wondered what else was out there.
What else I might feel.
Who else I could be.

The morning after came with consequences—
awkward, itchy, unforgettable ones.
I flew home, heart pounding,
and told the truth the best way I knew how.

We broke up.
Then we got back together.
Then the circle repeated—
with its strange kind of symmetry,
its hurt wrapped in familiarity.

It wasn't toxic.
But it wasn't healthy either.

Older Me,
I know you still carry some guilt from that chapter.
The should-haves.
The why-didn't-I's.
The confusion of feeling both loved and unsure.

But here's what I've learned since:
Love, real love, isn't a loop of mistakes you try to outrun.
It doesn't punish you for being young,
or curious,
or human.

You weren't broken.
You weren't even searching.
Learning.
Testing the shape of your own fate,
your own identity.

You didn't betray love.
You just outgrew one version of it.
And no matter how messy the path looked—
you still made it here.

Whole.
Wiser.
And ready for the kind of love
that doesn't ask you to trade your truth for comfort.

Still growing,
Love from, Your Younger Self

Dear Older Me, I Knew the First Day

I was supposed to feel proud.
Excited.
Grown-up.

New city.
New school.
New chapter.

Everyone kept telling me this was a big step.
The right step.
The beginning of everything I had worked for.

But I knew the truth the first day.
I wasn't ready.
Not for this program.
Not for this place.
Not to be that far from home, all alone,
with too little food,
too little space,
and way too much pressure.

I tried to talk myself into it.
Tried to smile and fake "fine."
Tried to act like I was strong enough to push through.
But inside—I felt empty.
Unseen.
Wrong.

Still, I let Mom fly in and walk me back to class.
I let the guilt speak louder than my own knowing.
I tried again.

Three months later, I walked away for good.
No drama.

No explosions.
Just a quiet, heavy choice that I *finally* let be mine.

And I never regretted quitting.

I only wished I had trusted myself the first time.

Older Me—
you've always been brave.
But sometimes you forget that leaving *is* brave too.
That it takes just as much strength to walk away from
something that isn't right
as it does to stay and push through.

You weren't a failure.
You were finally listening to your soul.
You were finally learning to choose peace over pressure.
Truth over expectation.

And that was the beginning of something beautiful:

You stopped letting other people's dreams define your worth.
You stopped mistaking persistence for alignment.
You started hearing your own voice again.

So if you're ever standing at a crossroads, wondering if it's
okay to change your mind,
wondering if it's okay to choose something different—

remember me.

I did.
And we're still here.

Free,
Love from, Your Younger Self

Dear Older Me, I Let Myself Fall—And I Don't Regret It

Under the statue of David.
In the backseat of a car.
In Florence, Italy.
Miles away from everything I knew.
Nineteen.
Single.
And spellbound by someone I'd only just met.

We didn't speak the same language,
but somehow—
we understood each other.
His English was broken.
My Italian was nonexistent.
But the way he looked at me?
That needed no translation.

We danced.
I lip-synced every American song like I owned the stage.
He laughed.
I laughed.
And for two nights, I wasn't anyone's daughter,
anyone's ex,
anyone's responsibility.
I was just *me*.
Alive.
Desired.
Free.

He drove me through the city,
pointing at monuments,
telling me their names with pride.
And I listened—
not just to the words I could barely understand,

but to the feeling of being seen.
Cherished.
Safe in the arms of a stranger who made me feel known.

Older Me—
don't let the world make you ashamed of that night.
It wasn't reckless.
It was sacred.
A moment of beauty in a world that often rushes past it.

No regrets.
No promises.
Just a memory etched in moonlight,
and a version of me that dared to follow her heart
across oceans and time zones.

You didn't lose yourself that night.
You found a part of you—
the one who still believes in magic,
in connection without words,
in love that arrives without warning
and leaves only tenderness behind.

Still dancing in memory,
Love from, Your Younger Self

Dear Older Me, I Almost Gave It All Away—But I Didn't

That summer, I was nineteen—
and completely swept off my feet.
He was smooth, successful,
older in the ways that made me feel like a grown woman.
Lebanese.
Charming.
Confident.
The kind of man who turned heads when we walked into the
room.

Every weekend, we danced at his uncle's club.
People smiled at me, served me first, treated me like I
mattered—
because I was *his* girl.
He had a nice car.
A good job.
An apartment that looked like something out of a movie.

And for a while,
I believed what he said.
That he knew best.
That love meant compromise—
even if that meant changing my life,
even if that meant getting pregnant
just so his parents would accept me.

I almost did it.
Moved to Calgary.
Gave up everything just to be enough for someone else's world.
But one week before I was supposed to leave,
life gave me something else:
a workshop—*Keys to Prosperity*.

And one little exercise changed everything.
A checklist.
One hundred things I wanted in a partner.
He didn't even score 58%.
Not even close.
And suddenly… I could see.
All the places I had shrunk to fit.
All the red flags I had called passion.
All the control I had mistaken for care.

So I did the hardest thing—
I left.
He was furious.
Said he had bought an engagement ring.
Tried to make me feel small again.

But I had found my voice.

Older Me,
if you ever doubt your strength—remember this:
You walked away.
You said no to a life that would have cost you *you*.
You listened to something wiser than charm.
You chose truth over fantasy.
And even though it took a detour or two—
you made it back to yourself.

Still proud of us,
Love from, Your Younger Self

Dear Older Me, I Thought Familiar Meant Forever

After I let go of the one I thought I couldn't live without,
I reached back for something that once felt safe.
An old boyfriend.
The one who had been there through years of growing up.
He didn't come with the same red flags.
He had history with me.
Memories.
Comfort.
78% on the checklist—almost good enough.

It felt easier.
Like maybe we could just pick up where we left off.
And for a little while, I believed we could.
We moved in together.
Tried to make a life out of what was familiar.
But something in me had changed.

I didn't want to see the truth at first—
even when his mom and sister warned me.
Even when the signs were right there.

He still chose drinking over everything else.
Nights out without a word.
No "Do you want to come?"
No "Let's do this together."
Just… gone.

I waited.
Hoped he'd invite me in.
Include me in his world.
But he didn't.
And I couldn't pretend it didn't hurt.
That I didn't feel like an afterthought.

That I wasn't quietly becoming invisible in the life we were
supposed to be sharing.

So I did something even braver than going back.
I moved out.
Got my own place.
Chose myself.

Older Me—
If you ever look back on that chapter,
not with regret, but with a curious ache—
just remember:
You didn't fail.
You woke up.
You paid attention.
And you honored what you knew in your bones.

Not every good beginning makes for a good forever.
Some stories serve their purpose
by teaching us what love should *never* ask us to shrink for.

Still proud of that choice,
Love from, Your Younger Self

Dear Older Me, I Wasn't Looking for Love—But It Found Me Anyway

I had just broken someone's heart.
And mine, a little too.
Almost five years later—
that's a long time to believe you know what love is.
But deep down, I knew it wasn't right.
And walking away… it hurt,
but it also felt like breathing for the first time in months.

I wasn't looking for anything.
Not love.
Not answers.
Just space.

Then came the unexpected.
Not in the form of grand gestures or butterflies—
but laughter.
Ease.
A new circle of friends that felt strangely safe.

And in the middle of it all…
him.

There was something about him—
not loud or flashy,
just solid.
Grounded.
Like he knew exactly who he was
and didn't need to convince anyone else.

At first, he was just part of the group.
A friend of a cousin.

A familiar face I saw again and again
until one day, he became the face I looked for first.

It wasn't a thunderbolt.
It was a slow, steady remembering.
A quiet unfolding of something I didn't know I was missing
until I couldn't imagine life without it.

Older Me,
I'm so glad you trusted it.
Even when it felt too easy to be real.
Even when it showed up when you least expected.

Because sometimes the universe waits until you've let go—
until you're finally clear enough inside—
to send you someone *true*.

And that's what he is.
Not just your partner.
But your mirror.
Your anchor.
Your chosen.

So if you ever doubt the magic,
just remember how he showed up
not when you wanted love—
but when you were finally ready for it.

Still in awe,
Love from, Your Younger Self

Dear Older Me, I Didn't Know It Could Be This Good

He was a 98% match—
not just on paper, but in the quiet moments.
In the way he listened.
In the way he never tried to fix me—just made space for me to be.

Six months after meeting, we moved in together.
And somehow, every day really *did* get better.
Not in some perfect, polished way.
But in the kind of rhythm that makes you feel safe in your own skin.
The kind of partnership that makes you believe in real love again.

We liked the same music.
Laughed at the same dumb jokes.
Shared stories, dreams, quiet nights, and early mornings with ease.
It felt like coming home—
not to a place, but to a person.

And six months after that…
we said "I do."
Not because we had to.
Not because time was ticking.
But because when you know, you *really* know.

Older Me—
Don't forget the way it felt in the beginning.
The comfort.
The surprise.
The joy of waking up next to someone who sees you, fully,
and never flinches.

If life gets busy—
if time wears soft grooves into the everyday—
just pause and remember this:
You once dreamed of this kind of love.
And then you had the courage to choose it.

Still grateful,
Still all in,
Love from, Your Younger Self

Dear Older Me, I've Never Felt More Beautiful Than I Did That Day

Do you remember?

How the whole world seemed to pause—
just for us?

How everything—
the dress,
the music,
the way the sunlight caught the edge of my veil—
felt like it had been placed there by magic?

I've never felt more radiant.
Not just because of the gown or the flowers or the perfect
hair...
but because I was *seen*.
Completely.
Fully.
And loved for all of it.

He looked at me like I was everything.
And in that moment, I believed it.

Not the old stories about being too much.
Not the voices that questioned if I was lovable.
Not the past that tried to dim my worth.

All of that fell away.

Because on that day—
I knew I was chosen.
Not just by him,
but by life.

We laughed.
We danced.
We kissed under the stars.
And for once, I didn't worry about what came next.
I didn't overthink or second-guess.
I just *felt* everything.

Joy.
Safety.
Gratitude.
That sacred kind of love that doesn't need fixing or proving.
Only *presence.*

Older Me,
if you ever forget what it feels like to be adored,
to be the center of joy,
to believe in fairy tales again—

Remember that day.
Remember *you.*
Glowing. Radiant. Loved.

You didn't just look like a princess.
You *were* one.
And not because of the crown—
but because you let yourself be loved
without shrinking, apologizing, or hiding.

Still twirling,
Love from, Your Younger Self

Dear Older Me, I Said Yes... But Was It for Me?

Right after the wedding, I said no.

Not yet.
Not now.
Not until I feel more ready.

And that was honest.

But somewhere in the quiet moments between dishes and dreams,
between the warmth of being loved
and the fear of somehow losing it...

I changed my mind.

Or maybe I didn't.
Maybe I just said yes—
because I thought I *should.*
Because I believed love had to grow roots fast
or it might float away.

And maybe part of me hoped that becoming three
would make "us" even stronger.

Older Me,
I'm not writing this to judge the choice.
I'm writing to honor how complicated it was.

Yes, there was love.
Real love.
But there was also the fear of being forgotten,
of being left behind if I didn't keep pace
with the version of life he seemed so sure about.

You see, I didn't say yes to motherhood because I had it all
figured out.
I said yes
because something in me hoped that *becoming more*
would finally make me feel like *enough.*

And even if I didn't know it then,
that little soul chose me anyway.

Not because I was certain.
Not because I had a plan.
But because I had a heart that was wide open,
and a soul that was ready to stretch into something new.

So if you ever question that version of us—
if you wonder why we didn't feel more prepared,
or stronger, or surer—

Remember: Love doesn't always wait until you're ready.
Sometimes it shows up when you're soft and searching.
And that's okay, too.

Still learning,
Love from, Your Younger Self

Dear Older Me, You Were Allowed to Want Something Different

You could have just gone with it.
You almost did.
You loved him—
of course you did—
but something inside you whispered,
"Not there."

And that whisper wasn't fear.
It wasn't selfishness.
It was *truth.*

You didn't want the life that came with his plan.
Not because you loved him less,
but because you were finally learning to love *yourself* more.

You stood at a crossroads—
and for once, you didn't fold.
You didn't swallow your needs.
You didn't say "yes" to keep the peace while silencing your
own longing.

You spoke up.
And that changed everything.

Older Me,
do you remember how brave that was?

It wasn't about *winning.*
It wasn't about control.
It was about choosing a path that felt aligned,
then trusting love would meet you there.

And it did.
He did.
You figured it out—*together.*
Not by forcing,
but by listening.
By opening up space for a third option neither of you had seen
before.

That moment taught you something vital:

Real love isn't about sacrificing who you are.
It's about building a life where *both of you* get to thrive.

If you ever feel the pressure to shrink again,
to go along just to keep things easy—
remember this:

You didn't betray love by choosing differently.
You *deepened* it
by telling the truth.

Still steady,
Love from, Your Younger Self

Dear Older Me, I Birthed Love... And Then I Forgot How to Sleep

The moment they placed that tiny bundle on my chest—
I swear the universe paused.

Time folded in.
Tears rushed out.
And my heart cracked open in a way that would never fully
close again.

This was love.

Not the kind from fairy tales—
the kind that grabs you by the soul
and says,
"You'll never be the same."

But no one warned me about the nights.
The endless rocking,
the bouncing,
the walking in circles at 3am
with a baby whose cries wouldn't stop.

Colic.
Cracked nipples.
The aching loneliness that comes when the world sleeps
and you're still awake.

And just when I thought maybe—*maybe*—I was finding a
rhythm,
I saw that second pink line.

Another heartbeat.
Another miracle.
Another mountain.

I didn't even get to catch my breath.
They were born eleven months apart.

Back-to-back wonder and wildness.
No sleep.
No silence.
No pause between who I was
and who I was becoming.

Older Me, you carried all that.
And you *kept carrying.*

Through the nights.
Through the noise.
Through the stretch marks on your body and your soul.

You became a warrior disguised as a mother.
You held joy and exhaustion in the same arms.
And you did it again and again—even when it felt like you were
unraveling.

You never really went back to sleeping through the night, did
you?
Different reasons now.
Different noises in the dark.

But maybe that's the thing:
You were never meant to go back.
You were meant to grow forward.

And I just want to say—I see you.
Still rising. Still loving.

Even if you pee five times a night now.

**Still standing (barefoot, in a messy kitchen),
Love from, Your Younger Self**

Dear Older Me, You Did It All... But Who Took Care of You?

I remember her.

The woman who had babies on her hip
and a business plan in her hand.

The one who packed lunches,
wiped tears,
paid invoices,
and stayed up late designing signs,
balancing budgets,
or just... catching her breath
after everyone else was asleep.

She was always *doing*—
for clients, for kids, for the future.

She believed in possibility
but didn't always believe in rest.

I remember how she second-guessed herself.
Was she working too much?
Was she present enough?
Was it okay to want *more*
when she already had so much?

Some days she nailed it.
Other days, she felt like a failure in both worlds.

But what no one saw—what *you* sometimes forget—
is how powerful she really was.

Because she kept going.
Not because she had to,

but because she *chose* to build something
that could hold the dreams of her whole family—
and still make space for her own.

Older Me,
please don't forget her.
Not just the effort,
but the courage.
The grit.
The grace.

She didn't wait for the perfect moment.
She *made* it happen—while making dinner,
and making magic out of exhaustion.

And even when the world didn't applaud,
even when the kids were too young to understand,
even when clients underpaid and the fridge was half-empty…

She was becoming a version of you
that knew how to juggle fire and never drop the love.

So if you're ever feeling behind,
tired,
or like you've somehow lost your spark—

Just remember the one who built an empire
with sticky fingers tugging at her sleeves
and a fire in her soul no nap could put out.

Still building,
Love from, Your Younger Self

Dear Older Me, This Wasn't the Dream... But It Was the Beginning

I didn't picture this.

Not the worn floor beneath my feet.
Not the paper-thin walls where arguments leaked through like wind.
Not the smell of old carpet and desperation.
Not the trailer.
Not the shame.

I remember feeling like the world was divided—
those who *had* and those who were *stuck*.
And I knew which side I was on.

It wasn't about stuff.
It was about *dignity*.

I wanted space.
Privacy.
Possibility.

But instead, I got *survival*.

Older Me, I know you've tried to forget this chapter—
or at least blur the edges of it.
But I need you to remember what it taught us.

We learned how to stretch a dollar and our imagination.
How to keep a dream alive in cramped quarters.
How to find magic in secondhand things.
How to appreciate sunlight through the smallest window.

And I need you to know:
You didn't fail.
You didn't "end up" there.
That was never the end.

You *began* there.
In grit.
In longing.
In hope that sounded like, *"Someday, I'll make this different."*

And guess what?

You did.

Maybe not all at once.
Maybe not in the way they write about in books.
But piece by piece, you built something real.
You created light where there had been corners of shadow.
You gave us more.
You became more.

So when life doesn't look how you imagined,
don't forget:
you've risen before.
From less than this.
With less than this.

And that girl who once whispered *"There's gotta be more…"*
is still cheering for you now.

Still dreaming,
Love from, Your Younger Self

Dear Older Me, I Thought I Might Lose Her Before I Even Got to Know Her

She wasn't planned.
In fact, I got pregnant with an IUD in place.
Eleven months after her sibling was born,
my body was still finding its rhythm—
and then, suddenly, it was carrying life again.

I didn't expect her.
But the moment I knew she was coming,
I loved her with my whole heart.

She came into this world fast—
forty-five minutes from the first real sign.
No epidural. No time.
And in that blur of pain and pressure and urgency,
the doctor's tone shifted.
She said, "Stop."

I saw the cord.
I heard the silence.
And then I screamed—
not words, just *instinct*.
Save my baby.

Everything exploded into motion.
Alarms.
Rushing feet.
Hands pulling and voices calling.
She had no air for six minutes.

I will never forget the gentlest touch on my shoulder,
the whisper that broke through my panic:
"I need you to push now."
I found something in me I didn't know I had.

When they rushed her out of the room,
I told my husband through tears,
"It's a girl."
And then I waited—
not just to hold her,
but to know if I *could.*

Eventually, she was placed in my arms.
And everything inside me exhaled.

Older Me,
I want you to remember this:
You were brave.
She was braver.
And every day since, you've been entrusted with the miracle
you once nearly lost.

She didn't come easily.
She came fiercely.
And even now,
she carries that fight, that light,
that second chance at breath.

Honor that.
Honor her.
And always, always know—
she chose you for a reason.

Still in awe,
Love from, Your Younger Self

Dear Older Me, I Know Why You're in Therapy Now

I saw you in that waiting room.
Holding back tears.

You told them it was "just for support"—
but I know better.

You weren't just there for your children.
You were there for *me*, too.

Because being a parent doesn't just bring joy.
It brings shadows.
It wakes the ghosts.

Suddenly, the way Dad slammed the door…
the way he yelled too close…
the way he made you cry—

all of it came back.

You remembered things you worked so hard to forget.
And this time, you didn't look away.

Older Me, I'm proud of you.

You didn't pretend it never happened.
You didn't say, "Well, I turned out fine."
You walked into that room
and said, *"This ends with me."*

You saw what you didn't want to become.
And instead of fear,
you chose healing.

You listened to that little voice—the one that had been ignored.
You hugged your children the way you should've been hugged.
You broke the silence.

And do you know what else you broke?

The pattern.
The legacy of pain.
The generational weight that told you love had to hurt.

Older Me, I know therapy wasn't easy.
I know there were moments you wanted to run.
But you stayed.
You spoke.
You softened.

And I've never felt safer in your arms.

So if you're ever wondering whether it mattered—
It did.

You saved us both.

Still healing,
Love from, Your Younger Self

Dear Older Me, The Day You Finally Turned Toward Yourself

I felt it the moment you made the decision.
That quiet, trembling yes.

Not the loud kind the world applauds.
Not the practical kind your family hoped for.
But the kind that came from the deep-down place.
The place where your soul had been tapping for years,
whispering:

"You were made for something else."

You didn't just switch careers.
You changed direction.
You turned toward *yourself.*

Away from what was safe.
Away from what was expected.
Away from the masks and into the mirror.

You stepped into the world of healing—
not just to help others,
but to finally meet the real you.

The one who always knew
that hands could carry light.
That intuition wasn't imaginary.
That the body remembers… and can be restored.

Older Me, I saw the way your eyes lit up.
The way you cried the first time you realized your presence
alone could calm someone's pain.
The way you finally understood:

"This… this is who I've always been."

You didn't get a map.
You didn't get permission.
You just followed the pull.

And because you did, you found a version of yourself
that school never taught,
and society never valued,
but *your soul never stopped believing in.*

So if you ever question the path—
if you wonder whether it was too late or too bold or too
strange—

remember this:
you didn't just change careers.
You came home to yourself.

Still shining,
Love from, Your Younger Self

Dear Older Me,
The First Time You Felt Energy—Before
Reiki Ever Found You

You hadn't even been initiated into Reiki yet.
That would come two years later.

But something happened that day.
Something you didn't have language for yet—but your body
knew it was real.

You were working at a natural health clinic. Your role was
emotional polarity work, but they were expanding what they
were teaching you.
You walked in one morning, thinking you were early—fifteen
minutes ahead, in fact—but the owner's father met you at the
door and said, "You're late."
No one had told you they'd changed your start time.

He led you briskly down the hallway to a treatment room.
And then—
There she was.

A woman, lying on the table. Her breast exposed.
He worked with women healing from mastectomies, but you
hadn't known you'd be learning bodywork that way.

He told you to stand on the other side of the table and gently
hold under her breast.
You were in shock. Unprepared.
So, you closed your eyes.

You were trying to disappear.
Trying to stay professional—yet felt completely out of place.

Then it happened.
With your eyes still shut, a *flash* of bright white light blazed
through your vision.
It wasn't from the room.
It was inside you.

You opened your eyes, startled. He was still working, unfazed.
You whispered, "I'm done."
He said, "No."
You said again, "I'm done."
He tested your arm—muscle testing—and finally agreed. "Go
wash up."

You did.
Hands shaking, door open, trying to clear the sick feeling rising
in your body.

He came in, washing his own hands beside you.
You told him you didn't feel well.
He said, "You'll have to learn not to take on other people's
energy. You have to get rid of it."
"How?" you asked.
"Go outside. Shake it off."

But you tried—and it didn't work.

That night, you prayed. A desperate prayer. A real one.
"Please—show me what to do. This feeling is too much."

In the middle of the night, something woke you.
You *knew* which book to find.
It was on your downstairs shelf. You hadn't even read it yet.

It was about chakras. And auras.

And in its pages, you found what you needed:
Salt water for clearing.

Energy sweeps through the body.
Imagining sparkling crystal light washing you clean.

You did what it said.
And it worked.

From that moment forward, you never took on someone else's
energy again.
You'd learned how to *hold space* without carrying the pain.
A skill that would become essential for everything you'd go on
to do.

You didn't know it at the time…
But that day, you were initiated.
Not with symbols or ceremony—
But with light.

Love from, Your Younger Self

Dear Older Me, When Trust Got Complicated

You wanted to believe him.
And you did.
But something still cracked.

It wasn't about the dance.
Or even the girl.

It was the *feeling*.

That split-second when he walked through the door and hugged you—
and in your mind's eye,
you saw what you *weren't* there to see.

And you couldn't unsee it.

That vision, real or imagined,
wasn't about whether he crossed a line.
It was about what rose up in you.

That ache.
That fear.
That ancient, buried belief:

"Maybe I'm not enough."

Older Me, I want to tell you something that no one else did back then:

That wasn't paranoia.
That was **knowing**.
That was your intuition refusing to go silent.

You didn't accuse.
You asked.
You gave space for truth.
And he gave it.

And even though it hurt—
not because of betrayal, but because of *what it touched inside
you*—
you stayed.

You chose conversation over collapse.
Truth over pretending.
Growth over withdrawal.

Do you know how rare that is?

You didn't shut your heart.
You let it stretch.

And what cracked open that day
was not just pain—
but the beginning of radical self-honesty.

That you could trust your gut *and* love someone at the same
time.
That your fears didn't make you broken.
They made you aware.
That love is not proven by perfection—
but by the willingness to face the hard parts together.

Older Me, I know you wondered if that moment changed you.
It did.

You got clearer.
Stronger.
More *you.*

And from that moment forward,
you stopped needing reassurance—
because you started trusting yourself again.

Still honest,
Love from, Your Younger Self

Dear Older Me, When the World Got Strange

You didn't ask for this.
You didn't even believe it was possible.

And yet—there it was.

That moment in your thirties when something *shifted*.
Clients came in for healing…
but you started seeing more than symptoms.
You felt what they didn't say.
You *heard* the silence between their words.
You sensed… someone else in the room.

A grandmother.
A brother.
A presence that lingered.

You told yourself it was stress.
Fatigue.
Your imagination.
But deep down, you knew:

Something was happening to you.
And it scared you.

You weren't trying to be psychic.
You weren't chasing ghosts.
You were just trying to help.

But suddenly, the veil wasn't just thin—it was open.
And no one had prepared you for what that would feel like.

The voices.
The visions.
The knowing.

You didn't tell anyone at first.
Because how could you explain something you didn't even
understand?

Older Me, I'm writing to remind you:
You weren't losing your mind.
You were gaining access.
You were opening.

It didn't come with glitter or angel choirs.
It came in the quiet, strange moments—
in goosebumps, tears, synchronicities, and messages you
couldn't explain.

That was your soul saying,

"You're ready now."

And you listened—
Even when you doubted.
Even when it felt too big.
Even when others didn't understand.

You stepped into the unknown anyway.
And in doing so, you cracked open the doorway
for others to heal more deeply
because you finally trusted what you *felt*.

You didn't become magical.
You remembered that you always were.

Still waking up with you,
Love from, Your Younger Self

Dear Older Me, When Weird Got Weirder

You thought you'd already seen strange.
But then... it *intensified*.

One day, you were sensing someone's grief—
the next, you could feel the energy in a room before anyone
spoke.
You saw flickers in the corners of your eyes.
You knew things you couldn't possibly know.
You heard whispers you never invited.

And suddenly, your body became a compass.
Your skin told the truth before your words did.
Your dreams were full of visitors.
Your intuition didn't just nudge—it roared.

You weren't just "in tune."
You were wide open.

So, naturally, you went back to where you were taught to seek
answers:
Religion.

You asked the hard questions.
You prayed.
You begged to know if this was darkness masquerading as
light—
or if the God you grew up with
was bigger than the walls you'd placed around Him.

But the answers... didn't come the way you expected.

They came *outside* the church.
In metaphysical books you'd once been warned about.
In crystals and energy fields and ancient wisdom that made your
whole being hum with "YES."
They came in Reiki attunements.
In past-life memories.
In strangers who knew your story before you'd spoken a word.

And for the first time in your life,
everything started to make sense.

Older Me—
You didn't abandon faith.
You expanded it.

You didn't reject your roots.
You let them reach deeper.

You found a path that honored both your knowing *and* your
wonder.
And though it looked nothing like the map you were handed as
a child—
it led you home.

So if you ever feel like you've "gone too far,"
or that no one will understand what you've become,
remember this:

You didn't go off the deep end.
You dove into the truth.

And I've been swimming with you ever since.

With reverence and awe,
Love from, Your Younger Self

Dear Older Me, When Hiding Wasn't an Option Anymore

There came a point where pretending just… stopped working.

You tried to be "normal."
Tried to be the quiet, grounded professional—
the reflexologist, the massage therapist, the wellness woman
with the proper intake forms and polite smile.

But then they started coming.

Not for the massage.
Not for the pressure points.

They came for… **something else.**

They didn't know how to ask for it—
not really.
But they could feel it.
That you saw what others couldn't.
That you *felt* what their words never said.
That in the quiet of the treatment room, something deeper was
happening.

And you tried to hide it.

You told yourself you imagined it.
You redirected. Stayed in the lines.
Tried to make yourself smaller than what your soul was
becoming.

But you couldn't do it anymore.

You couldn't ignore the energy dancing around you.
Couldn't pretend you weren't hearing their ancestors.
Couldn't keep calling it "coincidence" when it was clearly
calling.

So you did the unthinkable.

You stopped lying. You stopped playing small. You *left.*

You walked away from the safe structure.
You opened your own space—your own sanctuary—
where you didn't have to apologize for your gifts.

Where "woo-woo" wasn't whispered...
It was welcomed.

Older Me—
That was the moment you came out of hiding.

Not just professionally.
But spiritually.

And even though it was scary—
even though some people rolled their eyes or walked away—
you didn't.

You stood with your truth.
And that's what made room for others to stand in theirs.

You didn't just open a business.
You opened a portal.

And I've never been prouder.

With fierce alignment,
Love from, Your Younger Self

Dear Older Me, When the Door Was Closed… and Heaven Kicked It Open

You were finally ready.

You found the space.
Signed the lease.
Paid the money.
Told the universe, *"I'm doing this."*

But when you showed up at the city office to get your business license,

they said no.

Just like that.

No explanation that made sense.
No permission to proceed.
Just a cold, hard *denial.*

You stood there stunned,
clutching papers and plans,
wondering what you'd just done.

You'd already handed over the deposit.
You'd already told people this was *happening.*
You felt betrayed—by the system, by life, maybe even by Spirit.

But then—
just when your hope hit the floor…

Someone else walked in.
An official. A stranger. A messenger.

They looked at your file. Looked at you.
And said words that would rewrite your path:

"She can be a school here."

A *school?*

You hadn't planned on that.
You weren't even sure what it meant.
But something inside you stirred—
that deep, sacred "yes" that doesn't come from logic.

It came from somewhere else.
A higher place.
A wiser timeline.

You nodded.
Signed the paper.
Walked out with a school license—
and no idea *how* you were going to run one.

But you figured it out.
Because it wasn't your idea.

It was your calling.

Older Me—
That was divine intervention.

The universe rerouted your plan to deliver your purpose.
It didn't ask if you were ready.
It just opened the door and said,
"Walk through it. We've got you."

And you did.
You became the school.

The teacher.
The light.

And that moment?
It was the beginning of everything.

With reverence and wonder,
Love from, Your Younger Self

Dear Older Me,
The First Time You Taught a Class

You weren't officially a teacher yet—not in the way people expected.
But the city said if you were going to open a school, you had to actually *be* one.
So… you became one.

You started with what you had: a small space, a business license, and a deep well of knowledge you'd gathered through experience. You sat down and built a calendar of evening classes based on what you knew best—Reflexology. Intuition. Energy work.
Then you took a leap.
You placed an ad in the classifieds—the best way to spread the word at the time.
The class? "How to Draw an Aura."
The cost? Five dollars.

You arrived that evening wondering if anyone would even show up.
One student did.

Just one.

But you didn't cancel.
You didn't apologize.
You taught the class as if the room were full.
And in that moment, you became a teacher—not because of a certificate, but because you *showed up.*

And it was beautiful.

You shared what you knew.
You drew auras.

You held space for one person with the same heart and presence you'd one day give to hundreds.
And from that night forward, you just kept showing up.

Sometimes there were students, sometimes there weren't.
But the ones who came?
They kept coming.
They brought friends.
They told others.
And eventually… many came.

That tiny class with one curious soul started it all.
Because you had the courage to believe that your voice, your knowledge, your path—were worthy of being shared.

And look where it led you.

With pride,
Love from, Your Younger Self

Dear Older Me,
The Reading I Wasn't Meant to Give

It was soon after I'd taken my very first program on intuition and reading energy.
I had been desperate to understand what was happening to me— the sensations, the visions, the knowing that seemed to come from nowhere.

After the course, I decided to practice.
I put an ad in the classifieds:
Psychic Readings by Donation.

Clients came quickly.
The experiences were incredible—confirmation after confirmation.
Each person brought something new to learn, to feel, to navigate.

But then there was *him*.
A man who came in one day for a reading.

I started like I always did—
Closed my eyes. Took a breath. Tuned in.
Then asked Spirit for proof.
"Show me something about him when he was five."

I saw something. I said what I saw.
He shook his head. "No."

I tried again.
Nothing.
Tried a third time. Still wrong.

I stood up, ready to admit it wasn't working.
But he reached for my hand and gently motioned for me to sit back down.

"You can't see anything, can you?" he asked.
"No," I replied honestly.
He leaned forward. "You can't see the rapes? The murders?"

I froze.

"No," I said again, quietly. "Nothing."

Then he told me his story.
He had been part of a cult.
One filled with darkness and pain—
And he had *just* gotten out.

That day, I learned something that changed me:
Spirit doesn't always reveal everything.
Sometimes, it protects.

Not just me—but *him* too.

He didn't need his past dragged back into the light.
He didn't need to be defined by it anymore.
That day wasn't about a psychic reading.
It was about *freedom*—for both of us.

He was free to move forward.
And I was reminded that this path I walk is not about power, or proving anything.
It's about trust.
And knowing that sometimes, not receiving the message *is* the message.

Love from, Your Younger Self

Dear Older Me,
The Message That Mended a Family

There was an elderly couple who used to come in regularly.
It was the husband I worked on—Reiki and Reflexology.
Kind. Gentle. Quiet.

Sometimes his wife would sit with us.
Other times, she'd stay home, and during those sessions, he'd
ask me questions—
about the afterlife, about what I believed.

I always answered with care.
Never assuming he had to believe what I believed.
Just offering what I knew: that there's more beyond this life.
That love doesn't end when the body does.

Then one day, he stopped coming.
I found out later he had passed—stomach cancer.

But that wasn't the end of the story.

A year later, his wife came into the shop alone.
And suddenly—he was there.
Not in body, but spirit.

He was persistent. Urgent. He *needed* to speak to her.
I hesitated. This had never happened with her before.
I didn't know how she would react.

I told her gently that her husband's spirit was here and wanted
to speak with her.
She went pale.
Then without a word, she turned and walked out the door.

Moments later, she returned—with her daughter,
who had just flown in from Europe.

They both came into the private room.
And I began relaying his words. His love. His messages.

She cried. Then hugged me tightly before leaving.

But it didn't stop there.

Days later, her daughter came back—
She wanted to talk with her father too.
So we did.

Then a few weeks later, the son came. And we connected again.

Years passed.

Then one day, the daughter returned.
She walked through my door, smiling, glowing—
And wrapped me in another hug.

She said that first day, the one when I spoke to her father,
changed everything for her and her mother.

They had never been close. They didn't know how to talk.
But after that day, they found a new relationship.
They healed something deep and old.

All because love found a way to speak again.

So, Dear Me—
Don't ever doubt the moments that feel too bold or too strange.
Sometimes they're the very moments that mend the heart of a
family.

Love from, Your Younger Self

Dear Older Me,
The Miracles That Followed

It was about a year after your first and second Reiki initiations.
You had begun to feel the energy deepen—move through your
hands more clearly, more purposefully.
But nothing prepared you for what started happening next.

You were working with a student one day.
She lay on the massage table as you gently placed your hands
near her ear.

You said something softly—just a casual remark, really.
But she jolted. "Say that again," she asked.
You did.

And then she started to cry.

"I haven't been able to hear out of that ear for years," she said.

You hadn't done anything special—just followed the energy.
But something had happened.
A shift. A release. A miracle.

That was only the beginning.

Another time, you were teaching a hands-on healing class.
Fourteen of you gathered around a client—someone you'd
worked with before. She lay clothed on the table while everyone
placed their hands where they felt called.

It wasn't scripted.
It wasn't a performance.
It was presence.

Each student followed their intuition, moving where needed.
And the next week, she returned to class with tears in her eyes.

She told you she had breast cancer.
She hadn't shared that before.
But her latest scan? It showed the tumor had turned to a kind of
goo.

You did one more session with her.
And weeks later, she came back with something even more
remarkable:

She was cancer free.

That wasn't the only time.

You've witnessed Hepatitis C vanish.
Chronic pain dissolve.
Trauma leave the body in silence and light.

You've held space for healings doctors couldn't explain.
And while you've never claimed to be the one *doing* the
healing—
You've known, without question, that something sacred moves
through your hands.

And it's not just about belief.
It's about being willing to witness. To trust. To serve.

Even now, when science can't explain it…
You remember what you've seen with your own eyes.

Love from, Your Younger Self

Dear Older Me,
The Day the Pots and Pans Spoke

Back then, word was beginning to spread.

You had been quietly practicing—developing your intuitive gifts, trusting the unseen, learning to read energy like a language that few others understood.

You didn't advertise yourself as psychic. You didn't need to. People simply *knew*.

One afternoon, you were out front in the retail space of the school when a girl walked in. She didn't browse. She didn't hesitate. She walked right up to you and said:

"I know what you can do."

She explained her father had lost his Rolex watch.
They'd looked everywhere. No luck.
They needed help.

You didn't ask for more details.
You simply took her hand and said, "Think that thought."

You closed your eyes.
What appeared to you wasn't a map or a flashing light—
It was pots and pans.

That's all you saw.
You told her.

She left without much of a response.

But about a week later, she returned.
This time, she handed you an envelope.

Inside: a $100 bill.

She said they'd been doing renovations when the watch
disappeared.
They had searched everywhere.
But after hearing what you said, they looked in the kitchen.

And there it was—
Right there with the pots and pans.

That moment wasn't about the money.
It was about validation.

You'd trusted what came through—no filter, no ego.
And it had led to something lost being found.

You never forgot that.
Because it reminded you:
Your intuition didn't need to shout or make sense to anyone.
It only needed to be trusted.

Love from, Your Younger Self

Dear Older Me,
The Banana Test

You were still questioning everything.

Even though you'd seen shifts in people, felt energy move, and experienced healing moments—there was always that little voice wondering:
"Is this real?"

You weren't alone.
There was a man who used to stop by the school every so often.
He didn't come for classes or sessions.
He came to *test* you.

Not in a malicious way—more like scientific curiosity.
He wanted proof. And honestly? So did you.

One day, he walked in holding three small sandwich bags, each filled with cooked rice.

"I blessed one," he said. "Which one?"

You took a breath, grounded yourself, and whispered a quiet prayer for clarity.
You muscle tested each bag.

"This one," you said.

You were right.

Then he handed you three pieces of banana.
"I did the same," he said. "Pick the one I blessed."

But this time, nothing tested strong.
You tried again. Still nothing.

He looked confused. "I blessed it the same way I did the rice."

You paused.
Then you remembered something you'd read once—
About how the *skin* of a banana can be toxic or energetically off.

So you asked him to peel them.

And when you tested again—this time, with the flesh of the fruit exposed—
You picked the right one.

That moment was simple, but profound.

Because it taught you that truth isn't always loud or obvious.
Sometimes, it hides just under the surface—waiting for you to ask the right question.

It reminded you to trust the process.
To honor your methods.
To stay curious.

And maybe most importantly—
That your gifts, even when questioned, know how to reveal what's real.

Love from, Your Younger Self

Dear Older Me, The Woman with Rosacea

She came in crying.

An older woman—elegant, well-dressed, and strikingly beautiful for her age—stood in the middle of my shop with tears in her eyes. Her face was red and inflamed. She told me her doctor had just said, **"You'll have rosacea for the rest of your life."**

I didn't even know what rosacea was.
(But I looked it up later.)

She wasn't here for a facial or to shop.
She was desperate—for help, for hope, for *something else*.

So, I took her into a private client room and had her stand up.
And I introduced her to the **body pendulum**—a form of muscle testing that uses your own body as the answer key.

I asked, "Is it curable?"
Her body swayed forward: **Yes.**

We tested the products in her purse—lotions, creams, nothing triggered.
Then we went through her daily routine—shampoo, makeup, a few items tested *yes* as contributors, but not as the root cause.

Then I asked, "Can *I* cure it?"
Her body said: **No.**

Next: "Is the cure in the front area of this building?"
Yes.

I had a small retail space up front, and a 91-year-old herbalist—
Old Bill, as I affectionately called him—rented space there,
selling supplements and dried herbs.

I asked her to follow me.
"Is it a book?" — No.
"A supplement?" — Yes.

I began testing in columns.
Three columns—first one tested strong.
Five shelves—bottom shelf.
Ten products—second from the left.

It was **apple cider vinegar.**

"Do you drink it?" — Yes.
"How much?" — A capful.
"How often?" — Once a day, for a week.

"Anything else?" — Yes.

Turns out, she needed to *wash her face* with it too.
Once a day. For the same week.

She followed every instruction.

And when she came back a week later,
her skin looked completely different—clearer, calmer.

A few weeks after that, the rosacea was **gone.**

She glowed.

A year later, I saw her in the mall.
Still glowing.
Still clear.

That day taught me something powerful:
The body knows.

Not just *my* body—but *theirs.*
Clients. Students. Strangers who walk in off the street.

And when we learn how to listen—
with honesty, neutrality, and trust—
it tells us exactly what it needs.

Miracles don't always come from medicine.
Sometimes, they come from a bottle of vinegar,
a muscle test,
and someone willing to believe there *might* be another way.

Love from, Your Younger Self

Dear Older Me,
The Man on the Phone

The phone rang at work—nothing unusual.
But the voice on the other end wasn't looking for a casual chat
or to book a class.

He said, **"I want a psychic reading from you, but only if you
can prove you're real."**

Before I could even respond, he added:
"Tell me what I look like."

I was used to skeptics by then.
In fact, I welcomed the challenge—it kept me sharp.
So I closed my eyes, took a slow, steady breath, and sent my
energy through the line like a thread of light.

I saw him.
Tall. Slender. Dark hair.
I told him exactly that.

Then he asked about his wife.
I did the same thing—tuned in, described her.
He paused.
Said, "Thank you."
And hung up.

An hour later, the door to the school opened—and in walked the
man from the phone.
And all I could say was,
"Wow. I was good."

He laughed, pulled out his wallet, and handed me a photo.
His wife. Exactly as I had described.

He said,
"Even better. You were *right on.*"

Moments like that don't just validate intuition.
They remind you that it's *not* imagination.
It's *connection.*
Energy is real. And when you trust it—when you learn to listen
without second-guessing—it will speak through you in the most
ordinary, extraordinary ways.

It's not about proving yourself.
It's about remembering what you're capable of.

And maybe, just maybe…
Helping someone else remember too.

Love from, Your Younger Self

Dear Older Me,
The Mother Who Wasn't Ready

She came in asking for a mediumship session.
She wanted to speak with her son who had passed.

I did what I always do—closed my eyes, took a deep breath,
and waited.
With mediumship, I've learned that the best connection comes
when the loved one is called clearly.
So I asked her to say his full name and birthdate aloud three
times.

Then I waited.
And what I saw surprised me.
A room—not a typical image, but one vivid and unmistakable.
A **bedroom with a fireplace**.

I told her what I saw.

Then the message came through.
"Let him go," I said gently.
"He needs to move on to the light."

She froze.
Then she got upset.
Stormed out—**without paying.**

I tried not to take it personally. I knew grief. I knew how
complicated it made everything.

A few days later, she returned—but this time yelling.
I was in the hallway shelving books when she started.
"You had no right to say what you said," she shouted, her
voice echoing with pain.
She ranted in front of others for nearly ten minutes.

I stood there quietly. Listened. Let her release what needed to come out.

Eventually, she left. But I never forgot her.

Then—almost a year later—she came back again.
But this time, not in anger.
This time, as a student.

She looked me in the eyes and said,
"I was so mad at you. How could you say that to a grieving mother?
But no one—no one—knew he slept in the family room.
And it had a fireplace."

That detail, small as it seemed, had cracked something open in her.
She enrolled in my intuitive training classes.
And somewhere along the way, she learned to speak to him herself.

Because here's the thing I've learned about spirit:
When someone passes, they don't truly leave us.
But they do need to move into the light.
It's only from that place of peace that real communication becomes clear.

When we hold on too tightly—whether through pain, guilt, or longing— we sometimes block the very connection we crave.

That mother taught me something too:
That timing matters. That grief has its own rhythm.
And that sometimes, the most loving thing we can do is speak a truth someone isn't ready to hear—
and hold space until they are.

Love from, Your Younger Self

Dear Older Me, You Built a School Without a Blueprint

Do you remember the moment you looked around—
and realized it wasn't just a business anymore?

There were real students.
Real teachers.
Real courses.
And somehow… you had become the center of it all.

You, who once doubted if you could even run a clinic—
now walking the halls of your own school.

No business degree.
No clear plan.
Just intuition, trust, and a relentless heart.

It didn't happen overnight.
At first, it was duct tape and vision boards.
Trial and error.
Hope and hustle.

But little by little, it took shape.
Word spread.
The right people showed up.
And you kept showing up too—
day after day, year after year.

Fourteen years.

Fourteen years of teaching, growing, adapting, evolving.
Of believing in others even when you still doubted yourself.

You created something sacred.
A place where people didn't just learn...
they awakened.

Older Me,
you didn't just run a business.
You built a legacy—
and you did it while still healing yourself.

That's no small thing.
That's not luck.
That's purpose, embodied.

So the next time you wonder if you've done enough...
if you're still "on path"...
remember:

You already changed lives.
You already built the thing others only dream about.
You answered a calling... and then became the answer for
someone else.

And just because that chapter closed,
doesn't mean your magic did.

With reverence,
Love from, Your Younger Self

Dear Older Me,
The Horse That Came Back

Twenty-one years after Sailor,
I found myself with another horse—
Dusty.
A hand taller than a pony,
but something about him felt so familiar.
His color.
His presence.
Almost like Sailor had returned in a softer frame.

How he came to us—well,
that's a story layered with magic.

My daughter adored him from the start.
But we quickly discovered—
Dusty didn't trust men.
My husband and son tried to ride,
but he'd resist, pull away.
His spirit gentled only in our presence—
mine, and my daughter's.

It wasn't just the horse that echoed my past.
The place where Dusty boarded—
that same property once belonged
to a friend from high school.
Back then, she had a horse named… Dusty.
And I used to ride with her.
Full circle?
Maybe.
Or something more.

But what I'll never forget is the dream.

One night, I saw him.
A First Nations man,
dressed in soft deerskin.
His wife behind him—silent, watchful.
He looked me in the eyes and said:
"Your horse needs you."

It stayed with me.
So the next day, after work,
we drove out as a family to check on Dusty.

He wasn't by the barn.
We had to walk deep into the ten acres.
And there—
we found him.

His leg torn open from barbed wire.
Bleeding.
Alone.

I don't know how long he'd been like that.
The couple who owned the property were divorcing.
No one was watching.
No one was caring.

But I came.

We could only visit on weekends—
the days short, the evenings dark.
But we showed up.
With apples and brushes and healing hands.

Yes, we relocated to a secure boarding facility, far from the
neglect he'd endured.

Older Me,
you answered a call that came not from a phone,

but from Spirit.
And Dusty,
like Sailor,
became another soul-animal who taught you
that connection doesn't always make sense on paper—
but it makes perfect sense in the heart.

Still listening to the whispers,
Love from, Your Younger Self

Dear Older Me, I Asked Spirit for a Sign—And Got a Stoplight Instead

We had outgrown the space.
Too many students, not enough room.
It was time to expand,
but I didn't know where to begin.

So I did what I always do
when the next step isn't clear—
I asked Spirit to guide me.

And then came the red light.
A long one.
Long enough for me to stop rushing,
look around,
and *see* the For Sale sign I'd somehow missed before.

A boarded-up old Red Rooster.
Not exactly the vision I had in mind for a school.
But something tugged at me.
I pulled in. Wrote down the number.
Called my realtor.

His reply?
"It's a knockdown. There's no key."
End of story.

But not for me.

That night,
whether it was a dream or a whisper from Spirit,
I was told to write a letter to the owners.
So I did.
And I asked my realtor to send it.

A few hours later—
we had a key.

The place wasn't hopeless—just tired.
It needed some love, some light, and a little renovation.
What it *really* needed was belief.

The next challenge?
Buying a commercial building.
We sat down with a banker,
who told us no.

But I didn't stop there.

I asked him,
"What would it take to make this a yes?"

And he told us.

So we went back to the owners and asked to rent it
for six months while we renovated.
They agreed.

We did *everything* the banker listed.
Every paper. Every box checked.
And then we walked back into his office—
not knowing if he'd follow through.

But he did.
The answer became yes.

Older Me—
never forget the power of asking.
Asking Spirit.
Asking people.
Asking questions no one else thinks to ask.

You turned a boarded-up building
into a home for learning, healing, and transformation.

You didn't just expand the school.
You expanded what was possible
because you *trusted*.

Still listening,
Still building,
Love from, Your Younger Self

Dear Older Me, I Thought the Hard Part Was Behind Me

We bought the land.
That alone felt like a miracle.
Mom helped—after some nudging from my uncle—
and I thought the hardest part was over.
But I was wrong.

Building a house?
That's not like buying one.
It was a different kind of mountain.

Every step brought new questions,
new rules, new forms—
things no one tells you when you dream of a home.
I felt like I was climbing blind.

I even dreamed it once—
a house being built into the side of a mountain.
I had to scale rocks and scaffolding just to get inside.
And when I finally made it,
there was a man already standing in the hallway.
I stared at him, stunned, and asked,
"How did *you* get in?"
He smiled and said,
"Through the front door."

That dream stuck with me.

Because *of course* it's easy when you've done it before.
When you know the way.
When the doors open automatically.

But when it's your first time,
when you're just trying to figure it out…
it feels like climbing cliffs.

Older Me—
remember that part?
How the answers came in their own timing?
How one day a woman walked into your space,
not knowing she held the key?
You asked her what she did for a living,
and she said, "Mortgage broker."

And just like that—
doors opened.
Because you had the courage to ask.
Because you *trusted* the dream.
Because you kept climbing, even when it felt impossible.

Let this remind you:
Every expert was once a beginner.
And every mountain has a way up—
even if it's not through the front door.

Still building,
Love from, Your Younger Self

Dear Future Me,
The One Standing in the Light

There's a vision I've carried for years—one I haven't yet lived, but still lives in me.

It came first in a dream.
I was standing on a stage, high above a crowd I couldn't quite see clearly—only the sense of magnitude. There were balconies above me, rows upon rows of people below. I could feel their attention like a current in the air. Every eye was on me.

I wasn't nervous. I wasn't performing.
I was *transmitting*. Something sacred. Something true.

I was wearing a soft peach gown, flowing and graceful, and I looked older than I was at the time of the dream—maybe fifty or sixty. My voice was steady, but the words didn't matter as much as the energy—I was floating, elevated, surrounded by something greater than myself.

The atmosphere vibrated with awe, and I knew deep in my soul: What I was saying mattered.

Years later, I watched a documentary on Tony Robbins. When the camera panned out to show the crowd—thousands of faces packed into an arena—I gasped.
That's it, I told my husband. *That's what I saw.*

He was speaking to 18,000 people.
And I had seen it long before I ever knew such a thing was even possible.

I don't know exactly when it will happen, or what words I'll be sharing when it does.
But I trust it's still waiting for me.

Not because I'm chasing fame.
But because I'm answering a call.

So if you're reading this, Future Me, from behind the curtain…
Or looking back after it's already happened—
I want you to pause. To smile.
To feel how long this dream has lived inside you,
how many choices, lessons, and leaps it took to get there.

And then step out in full light.
Not just to speak—but to shine.
Because this was never just about being seen—
It was about showing others what's possible.

With unwavering belief,
Love from, Your Younger Self

Dear Older Me, The Castle Was Real

You always said the dream lived in your bones.
You didn't just want a house or a business—
You wanted **a castle.**
A sanctuary.
A sacred space for healing, learning, and becoming.

Most people would've laughed it off.
Called it fantasy.
Too big. Too unrealistic.
But you felt it.
Not just in your heart—but in your cells.

And one day…
there it was.

A real castle.
Just over an hour away.
Waiting.

The owner wanted someone to take it over.
You wanted the dream.
And for a moment—**you had it.**

The school moved in.
Your heart expanded to fit stone walls and soaring ceilings.
You saw students walk through the doors like they were
crossing a threshold into their own greatness.
You watched your dream come alive.

But then…

Reality crept in.

Big space. Big bills.
A husband who didn't love it there.
A family divided.

He moved back with your youngest.
You stayed—holding space, holding students, holding the dream—
until that final group graduated.

You left the castle with heartbreak and debt,
but not failure.

Because you tried.
You dared.
You *lived* the dream most would only ever sketch in notebooks.

Older Me,
sometimes the soul has to chase the wild dream
not because it will last—
but because it needed to be *remembered.*

That part of you?
The one who believes in magic, miracles, and sacred spaces?
She's still in there.

And the castle?

It may be gone.
But the woman who *built* her life around a dream...
she's still standing.

**Crown slightly tilted,
Love from, Your Younger Self**

Dear Older Me, I Came Home—But I Dreamed Even Bigger

We came back—
to my hometown,
to the man I loved,
to the house that held our life together.

But I wasn't done building.

The school needed more space again.
More room for dreams to stretch their legs.
And when I found the building,
I knew—it wasn't perfect on the outside,
but the bones were beautiful.

It needed work—
$150,000 worth of it.
But inside?
It was full of possibility.

Four spa rooms.
Multiple bathrooms.
A laundry room so big it could breathe.
A bright lunchroom where students shared more than food—
they shared laughter, ideas, support.

The classroom was our largest yet—
big enough to hold every question, every breakthrough.

And then we built the café.
served tea, snacks and lunches.
We didn't just teach healing—we taught business, too.
how to manage clients,
how to serve with presence and soul.

The first five years were magic.
It was the most complete the school had ever felt.
Like we had woven heart and hustle together in one place.

But even then,
something inside whispered…

"Go bigger."

Older Me—
You've always had the courage to start again.
To listen when the dream outgrew the walls.
You didn't settle.
You expanded.

You've made each move not just with ambition,
but with purpose.

Never forget—
you weren't just building a school.
You were building a legacy.

Still dreaming,
Still growing,
Love from, Your Younger Self

Dear Older Me, You Tried Again Anyway

You could have stopped after the first school.
You had already done the impossible—turned intuition into
impact, a dream into brick and mortar.

But something in you wasn't finished yet.

So you packed your vision, your courage, and everything you'd
learned,
and took it to the big city.

Vancouver.
Three million people.
One of the most expensive places to breathe, let alone build.

But you believed—again.
That lightning could strike twice.
That your second school would thrive, just like the first.

You signed the lease.
You smiled for the pictures.
You whispered promises to your future students.

And then…

You waited.

And waited.

And waited.

Because in a city bursting with people, somehow, ten more
never came.
Not like they did in the smaller town where heart, not
population, filled classrooms.

Bills stacked.
Hope wavered.
Reality landed hard.

But here's the thing you need to remember:

You weren't wrong for opening a second school.
You weren't foolish or naïve.
You were *brave*.

You followed the call of your soul, not the crowd.
You bet on yourself again, knowing full well the cost.

Older Me,
sometimes success isn't about whether something lasts—
it's about whether it changed you.

And this did.

You became stronger, smarter, clearer.
You learned what works, and what no longer serves.
You found that your worth was never tied to square footage or
city lights.

So don't carry regret.

Carry wisdom.

Because the second school?
It wasn't a failure.
It was a refining fire.

And you walked out of it even more aligned with who you're
here to be.

Still proud of you,
Love from, Your Younger Self

Dear Older Me,
He Was Always Brilliant—Even When
the Path Bent

He finished high school with *both* the English and the French
Dogwood diplomas—
top of his class and a letter that said:

*"Congratulations, you've been chosen from hundreds for the
Physics-Engineering cohort at U B C."*

It wasn't the easy route; admission was razor-thin.
He could have stayed in the Okanagan with his friends,
but the bigger challenge in Vancouver called to him—and we
cheered.

By third year the shine had dulled.
He called home, weary, talking about quitting.
I did what every generation tries to do for the next:
offered love, and a reality check—
"If you leave, you'll need a job and rent money."
So he pushed on, splitting fourth year in two.

Fifth year: our second school had just opened in Vancouver,
and he moved back in with us.
One evening he said a robotics course was tripping him up,
so I sat beside him, learned the syntax, helped debug his code.
(I still remember the rush—seeing arrays, sensors, and
armatures come alive.)

What I didn't know then?
He had already withdrawn.
Ninety-thousand tuition dollars gone,
and he hadn't found the words to tell us.

In that moment I saw the echo:
he was replaying my own story of quitting a program that no
longer fit,
and I was replaying Mom's—trying to steady a dream for a
child who'd outgrown it.

Older Me—
if doubt creeps in about whether you should have noticed
sooner,
remember the truth beneath the outcome:

- He earned two Dogwoods—the full academic spectrum,
  in two languages.
- He fought his way into one of the hardest programs in
  the province.
- He has never stopped being brilliant; the canvas just
  changed.

You didn't fail him.
You believed in him while he searched for a version of success
that felt like *his*.
And your love—unconditional, present, curious—remains the
constant he can still program his life by.

Still learning,
Still loving,
Love from, Your Younger Self

Dear Older Me, You Lost Everything— But Not Yourself

You thought moving provinces was just a change of scenery.
New city, new chance, same country.

But you didn't know.
No one warned you.

That borders inside a country can still divide you like oceans.
That contracts signed in one province don't always follow you
across another.
That promises—even ones made with hope—can cost you
everything.

You left that building in Vancouver thinking maybe—just
maybe—God was giving you an out.
He said, *"Just sign these papers."*
You thought it was closure.
Instead, it was a trap.

The landlord sued.
The governing body got involved.

And suddenly, your house—your home—was gone.
Your accounts frozen.
Your family, fractured.

No warning.
No protection.
Just silence and shame,
wrapped in legal terms and judgment you didn't deserve.

Boxes of student files,
a lifetime of effort,
and the hope that maybe… you could still make it work.

But they wouldn't let you.

They seized the house.
The bank accounts.
The future you had fought so hard to build.

But worst of all—
they took the thing you loved most.
Your right to teach.
To show up for your students.
To finish what you started.

You didn't walk away.
They pushed you out.
And that ache—the one of *not getting to say goodbye*—still
echoes, doesn't it?

Older Me,
I know you still carry some of that guilt.
Like you failed.
Like you broke something that can't be rebuilt.

But please listen:

Bankruptcy is not the same as brokenness.
You were cornered—
not careless.

You didn't quit—
you were crushed.

And still...
you rose.

You paid more than you owed—
in money, in dignity, in grief.
And somehow, you're still here.

So maybe this isn't a story about loss.
Maybe it's a story about *what remained.*

Your courage.
Your voice.
Your ability to create something from *nothing.*

That's the part they couldn't seize.

Still standing,
Love from, Your Younger Self

Dear Older Me, When You Crossed the Border—Again

You could've stayed bitter.
You could've curled into that small, broken version of
yourself—
the one who'd already lost too much,
too fast.

But instead…
You chose to grow.

You walked into massage therapy school not to prove anything
to anyone—
but because something inside you still believed in becoming.

You studied.
You learned.
You healed others, and in doing so, started healing pieces of
yourself.

And when you finally crossed back over that border…
hopeful, diploma in hand—
they looked you in the eye and told you it wasn't enough.

Not *their* enough.
Not *their* rules.

They said you had to choose.
Start over from scratch—again—
or surrender the rest of your brilliance.

And you chose *you*.

Not their boxes.
Not their gatekeeping.

You chose your gifts, your experience, your spa, your students, your path.

Because what they didn't understand was:
You're not just one title.
You are many.
A healer. A teacher. A guide. A force.

And what they couldn't take from you this time…
was your power to decide.

So you built again.
Not because they let you.
But because you remembered who you are.

You didn't fold.

You forged.

Still forging,
Love from, Your Younger Self

Dear Older Me, There's Always More— And You've Always Felt It

There's always been a whisper inside me—
a quiet pull that says, *This isn't it. There's more.*
More to become.
More to experience.
More to give.
And more to dream.

It's never been about being unsatisfied.
It's about knowing I wasn't meant to stay still.
Not spiritually.
Not emotionally.
Not in my vision of what life can be.

That whisper led me to many doors over the years—
and gratefully, I had someone beside me who believed in
opening them too.

In 2014, my husband and I enrolled in *Thinking Into Results*—
a coaching program created by Bob Proctor.
That course cracked something open.
It wasn't new information exactly—
I had studied these principles before—
but this time, I *felt* them.
It helped me rewrite old patterns passed down through
generations—
the ones that said *stay small, don't shine too much,
keep your dreams reasonable.*

Before that, we had taken T. Harv Eker's *Millionaire Mind
Intensive*—
another spark that showed us we were allowed to think
differently about money,

about abundance,
about success.

And years before that, I walked into an intuitive training
workshop with Cheryl Forrest.
That experience helped me trust the *more* I *felt* but couldn't
always explain.
The nudges.
The callings.
The flashes of knowing that would later guide my biggest leaps.

Each course, each retreat, each workbook and exercise—
they weren't just lessons.
They were *permission slips*
to grow beyond my past
and into the future I could almost see.

Luckily, I didn't walk those paths alone.
My husband and I, we've grown *together*.
We've done the work—individually and side by side.
Not always easily.
But always with the belief that this life is not a ceiling.
It's a launchpad.

So Older Me—
if there's ever a day you feel like dreaming is too big, too late,
too much—
remember this:

You were *made* for more.
And you've always known it.

Still dreaming forward,
Love from, Your Younger Self

Dear Older Me, When You Couldn't Save the Ones You Love

You've always been the strong one.
The one who shows up.
The one who *fixes things.*

But then came the moment you couldn't.

You saw someone you love unravel—
and no one would let you reach her.
They told you she was an adult.
They told you it wasn't your place.
They didn't see you at the window,
hands pressed against glass that wouldn't break.
Heart cracked open wide.

You weren't just watching her fall.
You were grieving what you couldn't do.

And still…
You loved her through it.
You loved her when the system didn't.
You loved her when you couldn't intervene,
and you loved her through the silence after.

You moved forward because there was no other choice.
But you carried the ache like a second heartbeat.

And when it broke you—
you let yourself fall into therapy.
You let someone hold you.
You let yourself name the pain.
You faced the ghosts in your family tree
and whispered their names in the dark.

You started to understand:
This wasn't just hers.
It wasn't just his.
It was woven through the bloodline,
quiet and unspoken.
And now it had a face you loved.

You didn't find all the answers.
But you started asking different questions.
You chose compassion over shame.
Understanding over blame.

And *that*, dear one,
is a healing that ripples forward.

Because even when you couldn't save her—
you saved yourself.

And that matters more than you know.

Still healing,
Love from, Your Younger Self

Dear Older Me,
I See Him in Him

I didn't expect it—
to be pulled back in time
just by the tilt of a head,
the flash of defiance in a child's eyes,
the way his feet stomped when the world felt unfair.

But there it was—
my grandson,
so much like my son.

The same fire.
The same ache beneath the noise.
The same wild, beautiful spirit
that didn't always fit into neat expectations.

I remember the days my son would act out—
the talking back, the refusal, the slammed doors.
And how tired I was.
How overwhelmed.
How I just wanted peace in the house
and quiet in my own head.

I didn't always know what he needed.
I just knew what the world expected of me as his mother.
Discipline. Order. Control.

But now… watching my grandson,
I see what I couldn't always see back then.

That sometimes acting out
isn't defiance.
It's a cry for safety.
For connection.

For a soft place to land
when the world inside feels too big to name.

Back then, I thought I was supposed to fix it—
to correct, redirect, contain.

Now I know better.

Now I sit beside him when the storm comes.
Now I listen without always needing to explain.
Now I remember my son's silence after the shouting,
and I choose to stay quiet with my grandson instead.

And sometimes I ache—
not just for them,
but for me.

For the mother I was,
doing her best in the chaos.
For the young boy who didn't know how to say,
"I'm not okay."

I wish I could go back
and hold us all a little more gently.

But what I can do now
is carry that knowing forward.

I can love the child in front of me
with the wisdom I've earned through time—
and love the child I once raised
with the forgiveness I've found in grace.

Because they're both in me now.
And so is the woman who sees them more clearly than ever
before.

Still learning.
Still softening.
Still loving,
Love from, Your Younger Self

Dear Older Me, I Chose My Name—And Finally, Myself

In 2017, after both hubby's parents had passed, I knew it was time.
For years I carried a name that wasn't mine.
Not really.
It had been a condition—*"I won't marry you if you don't take it,"* he'd said.
So I did.
Out of love, maybe.
Or compromise.
Or a mixture of both.

But after they were gone, I felt something shift.
There was no one left to offend.
No one to disappoint.
Only the whisper of truth I had tucked away for too long:
This isn't who I am.

I went searching.
Legally, spiritually, soulfully.
And what I found was…
home.

Not in a place.
But in a name.
One I didn't grow up with—
but somehow felt like it had always been mine.

Constance Amoraa Santego.
(Constance—yes, like the name my mother *almost* gave me.)
Amoraa—with the extra "a," not by accident but by intention.
Numerology made it an eight.
Strong. Sovereign. Whole.

And Santego… a name that sounded like freedom, like soul lineage, like destiny.

It wasn't just a name change.
It was a reclamation.
A rebirth.

I had to give up my original birth certificate.
Get my photo and fingerprints taken.
Visit lawyers, police stations, government offices.
But it was worth it.
Because when that new document arrived—
with my chosen name printed boldly across it—
I didn't just feel seen.
I felt *true*.

And when my daughter asked,
"Wait… are you still married to Dad?"
I laughed.
"Of course I am."

Because love doesn't live in a last name.
It lives in how we show up—fully, authentically, unapologetically.

So Older Me—if you ever feel lost,
if the world tries to label you something smaller,
remember this:

You chose you.
You let go of what no longer fit.
You honored the name your soul had been waiting for.
And in doing so,
you became *her*.

Still unfolding,
Love from, Your True Self

Dear Older Me,
I Thought She'd Always Be Honest With Me

We'd sold our house.
Had to wait a month before moving into the condo.
So we stayed with Mom and my stepdad—her third husband.
It was meant to be temporary, a pause between places.
But somewhere in that in-between… something broke.

It started small.
I thought I saw smoke once outside—wasn't sure.
But then I smelled it.
Confronted her.
She denied it.
"No, I quit after your grandfather died. I'd never."

But then I saw it again—with my husband beside me.
A cigarette in her hand.
We asked her directly, and without a word…
she shoved it in her pocket and walked away.

Later I saw a pack in her purse.
She said it was my sister's.
I asked my sister.
She said, *"She's been smoking for a long time."*

I couldn't believe it.
My mom—the woman who taught us that lying was one of the worst things you could do—
was lying to me.

A few days later, we went to my aunt's to play crib.
I laughed—out loud, free, happy.
And I heard her say something…

not kind.
The next day, I asked my mom not to bring us back there.
I cried as I told her what I'd heard.

She said, *"No… she wouldn't say that."*

But the next day?
She admitted she'd heard it too.

And just like that, another crack.
Because now she hadn't just lied to me once.
She lied again.

I wasn't angry that she was smoking.
I was hurt that she couldn't be honest.
That the one thing she always demanded from us as kids—
truth—
was something she wasn't giving me now.

I left.
Went to my daughter's.
It took me days to come back.
It took months before I said the words out loud:

"Why did you lie to me?
It's your house, your body, your choice.
You're a grown-up.
I wasn't mad that you smoked.
I was hurt that you couldn't tell me the truth."

That was the day I lost a piece of the pedestal I'd always kept
her on.
And I've wondered ever since:
What else wasn't true?
What else have I carried as fact that might not have been?

Older Me—
I know this one still stings.
But please remember:
Parents are human.
Flawed.
Frightened.
And sometimes more afraid of disappointing their children than
they ever let on.

You didn't lose your mom.
You saw her humanity.

And even when the truth falters—
your integrity doesn't.

Still standing in truth,
Love from, Your Younger Self

Dear Older Me, I Didn't Know My Body Could Break From a Broken Heart

It started at night.
Weird noises.
Waking up gasping—my breath caught somewhere between panic and paralysis.
I couldn't control the sounds coming from me.
They didn't even feel like mine.
I called them *episodes,*
but truthfully, I didn't know what they were.

Then they came during the day.
Worse.
More frequent.
And finally—hubby said *enough.*
"Go to the doctor."

I ended up in Emergency.
They ran bloodwork.
Hooked me up.
Checked my heart.

Hours later, the doctor walked in and said,
"Your heart looks great… but your blood sugar is 31."
(For context, it should've been around 4.)

I spent the night there.
Insulin shots in my hip.
All night.
By morning, I was down to 17.
Still high.
But they sent me home with a diagnosis and a prescription—
Metformin.

Just like that...
I was diabetic.

And I know what they'll say—
that it's genetics, or stress, or poor diet, or chance.
But I believe...
something else triggered it.

Something deeper.
Emotional.
Energetic.

It all started after my mom lied.
Not once—twice.
And not about something small.

The one person I had always believed would be truthful,
the one who taught *me* not to lie,
broke that sacred bond.

It felt like betrayal.
And not just from her—
but from my aunt, too.

In natural medicine, diabetes is often linked to love,
or the lack of it—
the sweetness of life turning bitter.
And suddenly, that made too much sense.

Older Me—
if you ever doubt that emotions live in the body,
let this remind you:
they do.
Truth wounds.
So does betrayal.
But so can love—
when it stops flowing the way you believed it always would.

You didn't make yourself sick.
But your heart cried out in the only language it knew—
and your body listened.

Still healing,
Love from, Your Younger Self

Dear Older Me, I Thought Education Would Be the Door

I was tired.
Tired of paying rent on another business.
Tired of carrying all the weight.
So I did what I thought was smart—
what I thought would change everything.
I went back to school.

Not just any school.
I committed to the big leap.
A Ph.D. and a Doctorate in Natural Medicine.
Years of learning, thousands of hours,
and over $40,000 invested in the dream.

And I did it.
I graduated.
I earned the title.
I felt… accomplished.

Until I found out something no one had warned me about:
That in Canada, those credentials meant nothing.
I couldn't use the title here.
Couldn't put "Dr." in front of my name.
Couldn't practice the way I thought I could.

It was a punch to the gut.

Older Me—
maybe sometimes you still carry the sting of that.
Maybe you still wonder if it was a waste.
But I need you to remember this:

It wasn't wasted.

You didn't walk away with just a piece of paper.
You walked away with knowledge.
With depth.
With a passion for healing that no law or policy can invalidate.

And you didn't stop there.
You used what you learned to teach,
to write,
to guide,
to change lives—
even without the letters on the door.

You kept going.
Not because of a title.
But because the truth of who you are
has never depended on permission.

Still learning,
Love from, Your Younger Self

Dear Older Me, I Never Stopped Writing—Even When No One Was Reading

It started in 2007.
That first book.
That first *royalty check*—thirty-seven cents.

Most would've laughed.
Some might've quit.
But not me.
Because that tiny check?
It meant I was a real author now.
Words in print.
A dream made tangible.

I didn't chase trends.
I chased truth.
I kept writing—year after year—
even when it felt like shouting into the void.

There were seasons of silence.
Of self-doubt.
Of wondering if the time, the effort, the heart I poured onto the page
was ever going to *matter*.

But I didn't stop.

And then—eighteen years later—
a book took off.
Then another.

Not because of a viral moment.
Not because of luck.

But because I kept showing up.
Kept crafting.
Kept believing there was someone, somewhere, who needed
what I had to say.

No, I'm not in the five-digit club yet.
But I'm close.
Closer than I've ever been.

Older Me,
If you ever find yourself forgetting how far you've come—
If you ever think it's taking too long,
or that the finish line keeps moving—
remember this:

Success isn't always sudden.
Sometimes, it's a slow bloom.
And you've planted a whole garden.

Keep writing.
Keep trusting the process.
Because stories have a life of their own—
and yours are just getting started.

Still writing,
Still rising,
Love from, Your Younger Self

Dear Older Me, I Chose Responsibility— But Left a Piece of My Heart Behind

We moved to Calgary—
not for adventure,
not for work,
but for love.

For family.
For our daughter.
For those precious grandbabies who still think I hung the moon.

For seven weeks,
I soaked up every hug,
every giggle,
every sleepy snuggle that didn't need words—
just presence.

But life has a way of reminding us:
love doesn't always pay the bills.

We tried to make it work.
We tried to sell the condo.
Tried to find jobs in the big city.

But starting over didn't match the life we'd built before.
Not in salary.
Not in rhythm.
Not in flow.

So we did what we had to do.
drove back
And got our stuff out of storage.

Back to comfort. Back to security. Back to money in hand.

And don't get me wrong—
I'm grateful.

Hubby's happy.
The numbers make sense again.

But sometimes,
I close my eyes and feel their little arms around my neck.
Hear the laughter down the hallway.
Feel the magic of being part of their everyday.

And I ache.

Older Me,
If ever you feel the distance too much,
if your arms feel too empty—
just remember why you chose this chapter.

It was never about giving up.
It was about giving *time*—to rebuild,
to find a way *back* that makes sense for everyone.

Because deep down,
you've always known—

Love like that?
It's worth working for.
And one day, you'll get to hold them again,
not just for a visit—
but for seasons.

Still missing the magic,
Still working toward more,
Love from, Your Younger Self

Dear Older Me,

We made it.

Not without scars.
Not without detours.
Not without breaking a few times along the way.
But we're here—heart still beating, soul still rising.

And looking back now, it's clear:
Every version of me helped carry us to this moment.
The girl who questioned everything.
The teen who longed to belong.
The woman who loved deeply, even when it hurt.
The mother who sacrificed and soared.
The dreamer who never stopped writing.
The seeker who always believed there was more.

Every chapter mattered.
Even the ones I wanted to rip out.
Even the ones I tried to forget.

We didn't always know the answers.
But we kept showing up.
Kept choosing love.
Kept choosing growth.

And maybe that's what this book really is—
a map of becoming.
A letter of reminders for the days you forget just how far you've come.
A thread connecting every younger version of you
to the woman who now stands in her power.

So when you feel lost again—
because you might—

flip back through these pages.
Listen to her voice.
Hold her close.
And remind her:

You've always been enough.
You've always been becoming.
And the best part is—you're not done yet.

Still writing,
Love from, Your Forever Becoming Self

Dear Future Me,

I wonder where you're sitting right now.
Is it in the hush of a private jet,
looking out over the clouds between cities and standing
ovations?

Or maybe you're barefoot on the sun-warmed tiles beside your
architectural dream home—
the pool glittering, the breeze soft,
peace woven into your skin like sunlight.

Wherever you are—
I want you to pause for a moment and *feel* this:

You did it.
You didn't just dream it.
You built it.
With every sleepless night, every step of faith,
every "yes" when no one was watching,
every "no" that protected your worth.

You turned your story—your scars, your lessons, your
healing—
into something sacred.
Into words that filled books.
Into teachings that filled hearts.
Into stages that filled amphitheaters.

But more than that, you became her.
The woman who walks with clarity.
Who leads with soul.
Who laughs fully and rests deeply.
Who lives in alignment with purpose and abundance—without
apology.

Remember when you were afraid to want too much?
To take up space?
To believe you could have success *and* softness,
wealth *and* wellness,
impact *and* intimacy?

Look around, Love.
You proved it's not only possible—
it's *yours*.

And if ever you find yourself dreaming new dreams—
ones even this version of us can't yet imagine—
don't hold back.
You've done the impossible before.
Now it's just a matter of what *more* you're ready to receive.

Stay magnetic.
Stay true.
Keep soaring.

With fierce love and boundless faith,
Love from, The You Who Believed First

Dear Reader,

If you've made it to this page,
thank you—from the depth of my being.
Not just for reading my story,
but for holding space for your own as you walked alongside
mine.

Maybe you saw pieces of yourself between the lines.
Moments that mirrored your own struggles.
Triumphs that stirred your hope.
Wounds you forgot still needed tending.
Dreams you thought were buried, but are still quietly breathing.

This wasn't just a book.
It was a remembering.
That we are never just one version of ourselves.
We are a thousand lifetimes folded into one lifetime.
And we are always becoming.

I didn't write this because I have it all figured out.
I wrote it because I'm still learning.
Still healing.
Still leaping, still falling, still rising.
Still daring to believe that it's never too late to rewrite the
ending.

So if there's something calling to you—
a path, a passion, a peace you haven't yet found—
let this book be your permission slip to go after it.

With love,
With faith,
With fire still in your bones—
Live your story like it matters.

Because it does.
And so do you.

With gratitude,
Constance

BIBLIOGRAPHY

Bibliography & References

- Eker, T. Harv. *Secrets of the Millionaire Mind*. HarperBusiness, 2005.
- Proctor, Bob & Leichter, Sandy Gallagher. *Thinking Into Results*. Proctor Gallagher Institute, 2012.
- Forrest, Cheryl. *Intuitive Training Program* (unpublished/private course materials).
- Government of British Columbia. *Name Change Process Overview*. "For more information on how to legally change your name, search 'name change process' along with your province or state on the internet or visit your local government's official website."

ABOUT THE AUTHOR

Dr. Constance Amoraa Santego is a natural medicine doctor, spiritual teacher, entrepreneur, and multi-published author who has spent decades helping others transform their pain into purpose. Known for her intuitive wisdom and unwavering belief in personal growth, she has built schools, written over forty books, and guided thousands of students through their own healing and awakening.

But before all of that, she was a teenage mother, a dreamer, a truth-seeker—someone who believed there had to be more to life.

This memoir is her most vulnerable work yet. Through real-life stories, raw moments, and powerful reflections, Constance invites readers into the sacred space between who we were, who we are, and who we're still becoming.

She lives in Canada with her husband and family, still dreaming, still creating, and still rising.

Message from the Author,
Dr. Constance Santego

If you're holding this book in your hands, thank you.

Thank you for walking through these pages with me—for listening to my stories, even the hard ones, and for allowing your heart to soften alongside mine. Writing this book wasn't easy. It meant returning to moments I'd long buried, truths I'd once avoided, and parts of myself I wasn't sure anyone would understand.

But I didn't write this for perfection.

I wrote it for **connection**.

For anyone who's ever questioned their worth, made a hard choice, lost their way, or dared to dream again—I see you. And I hope these words help you see yourself a little more clearly, too.

There's no single path to healing or growth or joy. But I believe that sharing our stories lights the way for others. If something here sparked a memory, gave you hope, or helped you breathe a little deeper, then this book has done its job.

I'm still walking my path. Still learning. Still dreaming of something more.

Wherever you are on your journey, I'm cheering you on.

With all my heart,
Constance Amoraa Santego

PLAY THE GAME *IKONA* – DISCOVER YOUR INNER GENIE

For additional information on

Constance Santego's

wide range of Motivational Products, Coaching Sessions,
Spiritual Retreats,
Live Events and Educational Programs

Go to

www.ConstanceSantego.ca

Follow on Instagram - Constance_Santego and
Facebook - constancesantegoo

Subscribe and receive Free Information and Meditations on my
YouTube Channel - Constance Santego